LEADERSHIP AIM

Align. Inspire. Measure.

EXECUTIVE COACH GLOBAL   ALINE AYOUB
MICHELE BUSH   SANDRA CABRAL
CRYSTAL-LEE OLSON   TANYA SMITH
ALEXANDER LUTCHIN   NANCE MACLEOD
WENDY WOODS   JULIE A. CHRISTIANSEN

Edited by
JULIE A. CHRISTIANSEN

Foreword by
RICHARD KOROSCIL

Leadership AIM

Align. Inspire. Measure.

Leadership AIM. Copyright ©2021 by Executive Coach Global. All rights reserved. Printed in Niagara Falls, Canada.

No part of this book shall be reproduced or transmitted in any form or by any means, electronic, mechanical, magnetic, photographic including photocopying, recording or by any information storage and retrieval system, without the prior written permission of the publisher except in the case of brief quotations embodied in critical articles and reviews. No patent liability is assumed with respect to the use of the information contained herein. Although every precaution has been taken in the preparation of this book, the publisher and authors assume no responsibility for errors or omissions. Neither is any liability assumed for damages resulting from the use of the information contained herein.

For information, address Executive Coach Global

Toronto Head Office

First Canadian Place

100 King Street West

Suite 5700

Toronto, ON. M5X 1C7

First print edition published 2021.

First E-Book edition published 2021.

Disclaimer:

This is a work of creative non-fiction. Names, characters, events, locales, and incidents are either the products of the contributors' imaginations or used in a fictitious manner. Any resemblance to actual persons living or dead, actual organizations or events is purely coincidental.

Designed by J. Christiansen. Created with Vellum.

ISBN #978-1-7775028-0-5

❀ Created with Vellum

CONTENTS

High Praise for Leadership AIM	1
Acknowledgments	5
Foreword	7
Introduction	11
1. Road Trip to Leadership	18
2. Surviving the Sharks in Suits	29
3. Leading with Empathy:	39
4. Unlearning Learned Behaviour	51
5. The Emotionally Aware Leader	62
6. Loving Leadership	76
7. Connection to Your Purpose and Your Why	90
8. Courageous Leadership	100
9. Getting Out of Your Own Way – The Practice of Leadership Flow	114
Re-Capping the Wisdom from Leadership AIM	125
Quotes from LeadershipAIM	141
References	147
Notes	151
About the Contributors	153
About Executive Coach Global	167

HIGH PRAISE FOR LEADERSHIP AIM

"This book is a refreshing telling of leadership where being authentic and achieving results are not mutually exclusive. Read this book and learn from the best." **C. Gallo, Director, Government of Canada**

"A MUST-READ FOR CURRENT AND ASPIRING LEADERS. THIS book will not only share the strategies and attitudes that are essential for all leaders to have, but it will provide you with actionable steps to make that enlightened leadership style a reality." **Marg Hachey, Managing Director, Ontario & Eastern Canada, GroYourBiz**

"STOPPING TO READ A BOOK LIKE THIS ALLOWS US TO SEE ourselves in a mirror to better reflect on our own situation and what we are doing. Real life examples from others helps to shed light on our own personal challenges. As I read this book, we are deep in the Pandemic's second wave. All the normal work stresses are there but amplified by a completely new environment. If you are feeling more stress and more out of control than ever then take the time to read this book, it will help put perspective in place and guide you to a calmer self." **Doug Lawson, Financial Advisor**

"THIS BOOK HAS BEEN WRITTEN WITH GREAT WISDOM OF experiences of top thought leaders in Canada. It is an easy, interesting read and a book I will be sharing with my leaders and keeping on my desk for future reference." **Bill Johnston, CEO, MBL-NA INC**

"AS I WAS READING THESE STORIES, I WAS IMPACTED BY THE vulnerability that was demonstrated; showing how their leadership styles evolved and how leaders need to be more adaptable. This book has definitely widened my lens in how I view leadership within myself and others. The moral of the story in general...we need to continue evolving what leadership means." **Mona Laham, Integral Developmental Coach**

"IF YOU ARE ONE OF THE MILLIONS OF ORGANIZATIONS across the globe who struggled to lead your team amidst a global pandemic, then not only is this is the book for you, but you are not alone! LeadershipAIM provides a 21st-century approach to leadership, with a clear understanding of the challenges that leaders face in a virtual world. Not only are the various leadership approaches relatable, but they provided strategic solutions to real-world challenges, resulting in leaders who thrive on cultivating a culture of success by starting with their most valuable asset, their people!" **Crystal D'Cunha, Chief Experience Officer, The INSIDE View Inc.**

. . .

"Everyone's leadership point of view is grounded in individual life experiences. This reads like a collection of stories; yet it is full of practical takeaways so we can all be better." **Neil Haveron, Founder and CEO, Haveron Leadership**

ACKNOWLEDGMENTS

Writing a book is challenging with many moving parts. I am sure those who have written books would agree this is a monumental task - it never seems to be finished - but somehow gets finished. This book could not have become a reality without the concerted and passionate participation of each contributing writer who have shared their stories from the heart.

In particular I want to thank Nance MacLeod, President of Executive Coach Global, for being the champion of this project and for bringing vision and focus to completing the book with inspiration, innovation and excellence. Julie Christiansen was our senior editor and publication coach who kept the writing team on track and guided us through the process from concept to publication. Thank you also to Richard Koroscil for his wisdom and writing the foreword, and to each copy reader who provided honest reviews which appear at the beginning of the book. Thank you to Crystal-Lee Olson and Lauri Richardson from our team for working behind the scenes in coordinating marketing language and strategy. Also many thanks to Artista Design and Print in

Niagara Falls, Canada for their support in assembling the cover and coordinating print publication.

I also want to thank you - our reader - for making LeadershipAIM part of your library and for sharing precious time with our amazing coaching and leadership development team. We have enjoyed the journey and hope you do as well.

Alexander Lutchin, CEO
Executive Coach Global

FOREWORD

My leadership journey began at a very early age as a Boy Scout in the 1960's in my hometown of Brampton Ontario. It was just after I completed my first year in the troop when my Scout Master, George McCallum pulled me aside at one of our meetings to ask me to be a Patrol Leader and lead a group of ten youths. He told me he thought I had the makings of an excellent leader. I wasn't sure what he saw exactly, but he explained it was the way I engaged and encouraged the other boys and helped the troop to focus on the task at hand. He said I would have to work on being a leader, that it would take time and that I'd make many mistakes along the way. However, he assured me he would be close by to coach and mentor me. He knew this would be an invaluable learning experience that would serve me well in my career.

I took on the Patrol Leader role with his support and I believe it set the foundation for a long career in leadership that included VP of Operations for Vancouver International Airport and Vancouver Airport Services, President & CEO of Hamilton International Airport, President of the Hamilton Chamber of Commerce and President of the Ontario

Chamber of Commerce to name a few. My leadership journey has spanned almost 60 years and taken me across the country and to many parts of the globe. And it all started with that astute Scout Leader who saw something in me as a youth and was willing to mentor me.

During my leadership journey, I have relied on the expertise of Executive Coach Global. I began working with them several years ago when I found myself in a position leading an organization with a workplace culture that needed improvements. The existing leadership team was technically strong; however, they were inexperienced and had been moved into leadership roles without any leadership training or coaching. It was clear to me there was much work to be done, and I knew we could not achieve it on our own. That is when I reached out to the experts at Executive Coach Global.

They undertook a comprehensive assessment of the organization and its workforce and provided the guidance and tools to build a road map. This road map assisted the leadership team and the rest of the organization in working together to achieve better results and improve the success of the business. The wealth of knowledge, skills, and experience, that Executive Coach Global provided to help us overcome our leadership challenges, are described here within the pages of this book.

This book presents a unique opportunity to experience the lessons of some exceptional leaders through a creative non-fiction tool in which each writer has adopted an avatar. Through the avatars they tell a story to share real leadership lessons and the results are evidence-based and true for each writer.

These leaders do not shy away from telling the real story, both the good and the bad. They show the reader how to learn from both experiences, how to replicate their positive experiences and learn from the negative ones. I'm sure, like me, readers will be able to see themselves in these stories. I have been in many of these situations over the years and certainly would have benefited from the wisdom offered in these pages. For those readers who are currently on their own leadership journey, these stories will provide important insights and learnings that will undoubtedly help you overcome the challenges you are sure to face in your career as a leader.

I know some people believe in the idea of natural born leaders. I doubt this is true. When I reflect on my leadership journey and look to the learnings in this book, it is apparent that leadership is about experimenting and learning from other leaders. Some leaders like my Scout Master and the experts at Executive Coach Global can teach us how to be a great leader; from others, we may learn what not to do as a leader.

You will also learn from this book that organizations and their leaders must understand the power of an engaged workforce. Engagement that comes from the alignment of purpose, inspirational leadership, and understanding and measuring success. An engaged workforce increases employee satisfaction, which results in better performance and a more successful business.

This book and its stories can help any leader, whether you are just embarking on your leadership journey or you are a seasoned leader; and whether you lead a workforce of many or just a few. You will learn how to create a work environment that engages and excites people. If you are a leader seeking guidance in overcoming challenges or simply looking for ways to be a better leader, you've picked up the right book!

Richard Koroscil

INTRODUCTION

> *"Be humble. Be hungry. And always be the hardest worker in the room."*
> Dwayne "The Rock" Johnson

Here's the Thing...
They say the best leaders are humble leaders. Being hungry is often seen as having the will and the determination to reach "the top" regardless of who may be crushed on your ascent to greatness. Being the hardest worker in the room has traditionally been interpreted to mean you work yourself to an early grave in exchange for material gain and accolades from your industry peers. What turns these notions on their ear is the first statement in Johnson's leadership philosophy: be humble.

The thing about leadership is this: too many people confuse the concept of leadership with that of management. You see, management is for systems, not for people. When you try to manage people, that is, when you treat people like just another cog in the wheel rather than a human being with opinions, thoughts, emotions, and free will, that is when things begin to go wrong.

Nothing has clarified this long-standing truth more than the global pandemic and the COVID19 crisis. One moment, we were rolling merrily along, engaging in business as usual. In the blink of an eye, the world of work had shifted. People were moving their computer equipment out of their offices or cubicles and into their homes. Boardrooms went virtual, as did schoolrooms, conferences, events, weddings, and even funerals. Whether we liked it or not, life as we knew it was changing.

Pivot or Perish

Seemingly overnight, all the things we took for granted – the processes, the systems, the supervision models that we believed to be best practice, no longer factored. Leaders and managers alike needed to pivot and adapt quickly in order to keep processes moving, people employed, and profits stable. Those unwilling or unable to change would perish under the new global conditions created by the pandemic.

The COVID19 crisis has shone a spotlight on challenges leaders have faced for decades, but many chose to ignore. The economic effects of a global pandemic have forced us to question old habits, established expectations, and faulty beliefs that hampered business growth both from the perspective of profitability as well as our people.

Leadership AIM represents over 200 years of cumulative leadership wisdom. Our goal for this book is that it will magnify the fundamental aspects that define the 21st Century leader – the ability to align people with purpose, to inspire and empower those people to fulfill their purpose by maximizing their potential, and to measure the ensuing results using parameters beyond a simple P and L report.

How to Maximize the Benefits of This Book

LEADERSHIP AIM

This team of exceptional leadership and executive coaches chose the vehicle of creative non-fiction as a tool to deliver the leadership lessons encapsulated in each chapter. As we brainstormed about what we hoped to accomplish with the content, and how we wanted it to be received, an image of avatars kept coming up in the discussion. Each of us adopted an avatar through which we could communicate our leadership lessons; taking the focus away from ourselves and pointing instead to the all-important messages embedded in each of our chapters. The use of story is intended to connect the reader's brains in a unique way, by engaging both sides of the brain (logical and creative; linear and multidirectional), thereby exemplifying the notion that "growth happens in all directions".

As you read through each chapter, it is essential that you remember that these stories are fictionalized accounts based on the cumulative professional experience of each contributor. The stories are not written in the voice of the author; rather, they are told through the voice of an avatar. For us, the word, 'avatar' represents the personification of a leader, embodying not only the fictionalized persona of each leader, but also a framework in which they undergo an evolution from their old style of leadership to one that is new and improved. Through their learnings, they become different versions of themselves.

Remember too, that as a work of creative non-fiction, any resemblance to real people or organizations is absolutely coincidental. I might suggest, however, that if you recognize yourself in the pages of this book, that you take each avatar's story as a cautionary tale. Learn from the stories that resonate and sound like your own, and give the actionable items they suggest the old college try.

This is not a book of "shoulds"; rather, it is a book of

"here's how". Each avatar has more than a story to tell. They share their experiences in order for you to put what they learned into context. Although the stories are fictionalized, the lessons are real, and the results attained are evidenced-based and true for each contributing author.

A Journey through Leadership AIM

First up, Sandra Cabral will invite you on a road trip to explore the meaning and value of Leadership AIM (Align, Inspire & Measure). She will introduce you to the Seven Fundamentals of Leadership. You will notice that the thread of the Seven Fundamentals is woven tightly throughout the pages of this book, even though each author/avatar writes from a different perspective on leadership.

Al Lutchin's avatar shares a journey that many of us in the world of work have experienced, one that is rife with danger due to "sharks in suits". His valuable advice will prepare and equip you for surviving the shark-infested waters of the business world, and he will introduce you to a coaching leadership style that is revolutionary for 21st century workplaces.

Aline Ayoub explores the value of empathy as a leadership trait. She tells a story of shifting from one leadership style into the growth and development of a new and improved avatar, one who appreciates non-tangible qualities like compassion and resiliency. She will demonstrate how to align the skills and strengths of her team with the rapidly changing world of work, in order for the team to pivot and profit.

Is it ever too late to unlearn learned behaviour? This is the question addressed by Michele Bush's character, who was working herself to the bone in the belief that pushing herself and others was the only way to get things done. New lessons learned will demonstrate the value of teamwork, engaging with your team as your partners rather than your subordinates, and how striving for a healthier work-life balance provides benefits for leaders, their families, friends, teams, and co-workers.

Wendy Woods's shares a journey in which her storyteller ignored and minimized emotions as having no place in the profile of a leader. She will demonstrate the value of developing one's emotional intelligence and provides the framework in which you can do the same. The emotionally intelligent leader is self-aware, is able to keep a more informed pulse on the morale and energy of the team, and as a result, will be able to build trust and enhance engagement.

In Loving Leadership, on the edge of a spectacular burnout, my fictionalized leader takes a walk on the wild side, and learns about a brand new leadership model while on a white water rafting trip. The leader comes to realize that trying to control everything results in having almost no control at all. His impromptu coach uses white water rafting as an extreme object lesson, demonstrating how educating, engaging, and trusting your team can turn the most risky of activities into an exhilarating, enjoyable expericnce. The avatar emerges from the trip having learned the value of intimacy, passion, and commitment in creating radically enthusiastic and engaged team members.

Crystal-Lee Olson's character comes to a place where she gets connected with her purpose as a leader. Attaining a greater understanding of her WHY enables her to engage more fully with her work; by extension, learning how to communicate the WHY to her team instills greater connection to the overall mission and vision of the organization, thereby inspiring deeper engagement. "Leadership is equivalent to an art form; like art, leadership is to produce work that inspires others and inspires change."

In Courageous Leadership, Nance MacLeod's avatar learns how to navigate the world of business leadership with the help of her mentor and coach. He shows her the value of criticism and resistance, teaches her how to leverage her skills and inherent talents to become a courageous leader. It is not uncommon for people in leadership roles to experience bouts of imposter syndrome, even after many years of trudging through the leadership trenches. This chapter highlights the power of persistence, self-awareness, authenticity; the value of being a good listener, and the benefits of being a lifelong learner.

Tanya Smith's character, Jackson, shares how his mentor helped him to get out of his own way, and to embrace the practice of "leadership flow". Learning the process of reflection, intention, and action introduces Jackson to a new way of interacting with his teams; one that engaged them in processes instead of imposing processes upon them. A detailed formula for practicing leadership flow is included in this chapter for you to apply and practice. Jackson's coach provides some key advice, which when applied, encapsulates the intention for this book on the whole: *Start Slow – try one new thing at a time and think about how it supports you. Be Kind to Yourself – this is key as you may be learning something new. Start Again –this is the most important rule; improvement/change will only come with practice, which grants you permission to start over.*

Each contributor to this book has a unique writing style, and each voice carries a unique perspective on leadership; however, you will find that there are many common threads that weave together the tapestry that is the final product. Themes of humility, trust, instilling a purpose, and inspiring passion in the human resources that are at the heart of every organization. Themes that encourage turning away from practices that act like fertilizer in a weed bed of negativity and toxic behaviours. Themes that encourage intangible skill sets like empathy, compassion, emotional intelligence, and servant leadership. Ensuring that teams are aligned with passion and purpose; that they are inspired to work together for each others' success as well as the success of the organization employing them; and, measuring both the quantitative and qualitative outcomes, is the tapestry we call Leadership AIM.

Julie A. Christiansen

I

ROAD TRIP TO LEADERSHIP

By Sandra Cabral

Some of my fondest childhood memories take place in a car. Sunday road trips, mystery tours. These adventures were family tradition, time to chat, time to see what the world had to offer. In those days, I was in the back seat with my sister, and my mom was co-pilot to my dad, the driver. On these drives there were no maps to follow. My parents made decisions about our direction as we drove. There was trust, respect, communication, and the confidence we would achieve our goals: travel new roads, experience new things, and have lunch at McDonalds.

A number of years later I would be the one driving the family car, my dad as a nervous but patient passenger, heading to our vacation spot. Of course, a lot happened since my sister and I were passengers in the back seat. As our independence grew, there were bumps along the way, which often required my parents to be flexible, adaptable, and recover quickly in order to be ready for the next hurdle.

It may be a surprise to you to learn that our actions did

LEADERSHIP AIM

not always meet expectations. We were held accountable. We were coached and mentored with meaningful conversations that allowed us to bridge the gaps and grow. Our leaders, our parents, achieved results beyond their expectations. They created a committed team that is resilient, a team that other teams aspire to mirror, a team they are extremely proud of.

You may be wondering how this recounting of my childhood is part of a book about leadership. My parents were my first great examples of leadership. I learned that leadership is not found in a title. It is found in a person's abilities and actions; a person's ability to align, inspire, and measure by consistently demonstrating the seven fundamentals of leadership and team engagement created by Executive Coach Global & Career Compass Canada. These seven fundamentals are: gaining trust, communicating for transparency, earning respect, building resilience, managing change, coaching with compassion, and achieving results.

MY FIRST SOLO ROAD TRIP BEGAN AS A TEN-DAY TEMPORARY assignment in a Human Resources Department which I had reluctantly accepted. My previous exposure to Human Resources had not been very pleasant however any job, even this one, was better than no job at all. So here I sat, at the front of the HR department; greeter, screener to all who would dare to enter. I soon found out that my assignment had come about as a result of a resignation. In fact, the department of eight was now a department of four. The HR leader, Steve was a brilliant labour relations professional. He took an interest in my professional development supporting continuing education and experience that allowed me to achieve my professional designation. I was provided with incredible opportunities to participate across all HR disciplines.

That ten-day assignment turned into three years and I am grateful, to this day, for this experience. Therefore, it may surprise you to hear that I do not consider Steve to have been a great or even a good leader. For example, twice weekly the management team would gather. At least once weekly during the break, Steve would return to HR red-faced and angry accusing one or more of the team members of something that had invariably made him look bad. Communication or lack thereof, was almost always the culprit and subsequently, there was no truth to the accusation however there was certainly a result, an erosion of trust. While he was called a leader, he did not understand what that meant. He failed in the first, and in my opinion, the most important leadership fundamental, gaining trust. Team member weaknesses were exploited, and mistakes were highlighted. Trust establishes the foundation of any relationship. Where trust is missing, there is no alignment and no inspiration. It is impossible to communicate effectively or transparently.

What is necessary to gain trust? According to Harvard Business Review[1], trust develops from focusing on "three core drivers: authenticity, logic, and empathy. People tend to trust you when they think they are interacting with the real you (authenticity), when they have faith in your judgment and competence (logic), and when they believe that you care about them (empathy). When trust is lost, it can almost always be traced back to a breakdown in one of these three drivers."

When employees feel they can't trust leadership they feel unsafe, and their focus moves to find their next job opportunity. This takes us back to my first day of work where a department of eight had recently become a department of four. The cycle was destined to repeat itself because nothing had changed. The HR department was left vulnerable and incapable of retaining employees.

That is not to say that I did not find amazing leadership within that same organization. About one year after joining, I accepted the position of Employee Relations Representative. It was my first leadership role, and I was responsible for 350 tradespersons. The thought of this was terrifying but exciting. During this transition from HR Admin to Employee Relations, I found myself in conversation with a millwright, Gary, and I expressed both my apprehension and excitement about my new position. His advice was simple: if you take the time to know the employees in their environment and to understand their perspectives, then they will see you as person instead of human resources. I took his advice and over a one-year period did exactly that. I invested the time, gained trust, communicated for transparency, and earned respect.

The next leadership lesson came from an unlikely source, Alex, the union President. We were working through pay equity, and it was my first time as chair of a committee. Alex brought a wealth of knowledge he had accumulated over 30 years to the table. To say the table was tilted in his direction was an understatement. He could have easily taken advantage of this, yet he chose a different path. With full committees at the table and at a pivotal point in the talks, Alex requested a sidebar with me. His advice was straightforward.

Alex suggested that listening is much more valuable than speaking. He suggested that thinking before speaking is much more valuable than speaking first. Alex went on to explain the motivation for his sidebar. He noticed I had not been listening, and because of that, I misunderstood a key point. My misunderstanding would have had a negative impact for the company and reflected poorly on me. This was a defining moment in my career. I followed his advice and, in the years that followed, our relationship was resilient, withstanding adversarial collective agreement negotiations, grievances, and differing positions based on our representations. We had established mutual trust and respect.

I have presented two very different experiences in the same organization. The difference in leadership was night and day and is easily explained. A key leadership fundamental is communicating for transparency. "Leaders who communicate well, build on trust and respect. Two-way communication is vital to ensure others feel listened to and valued. This is a core value that drives innovation and team development for retention and performance. It builds on trust and respect."[2]

The leadership Steve demonstrated was void of both trust and respect, whereas both values were found in the subsequent experiences. The relationship with Alex illustrates that respect is not about agreement, it is about listening. Jackie Robinson once said, "I'm not concerned with your liking or disliking me.....all I ask is that you respect me as a human being."[3] Simply put, respect is about having due regard for people's wishes, traditions, and values. Differences provide opportunities for both personal and professional growth.

My time with this organization ignited my passion for "people relations" in the workplace and significantly influenced my career decisions. People don't leave organizations, they leave the people in those organizations. They leave the leadership; they leave coworkers; they leave a culture that is not supportive of their values.

Positive culture facilitates optimal performance. Employees in these organizations are aligned and inspired to do their best. These employees welcome measurement and the recognition that comes with success. Positive culture is a direct result of effective leadership. Leaders that are authentic, logical and have empathy inspire the same behavior in others. A positive culture is made up of strong leaders and committed employees. A strong workforce is a resilient work-

LEADERSHIP AIM

force. In times of crisis and uncertainty the organizations that have this strength are the ones that survive.

Imagine then an environment where labour unrest was its notoriety. To set the stage, this organization had deep roots in the community. It was an "exclusive" workplace run by two parties: the manager of the facility and the union president. There had been a labour interruption at each collective agreement renewal for the last 20 years. There was no trust, no respect, no communication, no resilience, no openness to change, no coaching and subsequently, no results. They were on the brink of closure. It was for all of these reasons that I accepted a position as part of the new management team.

It takes years to build a positive culture and very little time to tear it down. The new leadership team had a small window of time in which to prove that the employees, the union, and the managers could succeed in changing the financial direction of the company. A complete turnaround was essential, and success had to come from the people. We needed actions to support the transformation.

As a Kaizen facilitator, I taught the value of incremental improvements. This was an opportunity to apply those methodologies. Our priority, as leaders, was to establish partnerships based on trust, respect, and communication for transparency. How we would accomplish this was through a five-step behavioral map:

1. **Be Present Not Just Seen.** Managers had always been expected to be present on the shop floor. In reality, they met this obligation by being seen; walking as quickly as possible with head down to avoid eye contact and any potential interaction. Being present, means to be involved and establish relationships.
2. **Listen & Learn.** Going back to my life lesson

about listening, this point was my contribution to our behavioral map to success. Leaders invested the time to listen and to learn. They brought knowledge to each other, sharing experiences, learning from the employees, their representatives, and each other.
3. **Act with Integrity.** Integrity is the act of behaving honorably even when no one is watching. Acting with integrity meant our decisions needed to follow moral and ethical principles that facilitated inclusion. In other words, taking the easy way out was not an option.
4. **Become a Coach, Develop a Team.** The leadership team seized coaching opportunities that supported the first steps towards developing a positive culture.
5. **Give and Receive Feedback.** Partnerships occur when two or more parties engage in the same activity. It happens when everyone is moving in the same direction.

The key to the success was that the leadership team held each other accountable.

This is not to suggest that during the next three years, the road to sustainability was a smooth one. Our workforce needed to be confident that we were open for business and that the strategies in place were designed to keep the employees and the company together. To accomplish this, we focused on creating pride amongst all partners. Our facility became recognizable in the community through fundraising activities that directly impacted the families surrounding our facility. Our employees became our proud ambassadors.

As our partnership strengthened, we were able to begin looking for opportunities to protect our business and to adapt our processes for sustainability. Our partnerships were resilient, overcoming economic disasters, strenuous negotiations and political influences that threatened our survival. The new management leadership team was now a partner with the new union committee, and an influx of new employees ensued.

However, managing all this change challenged us to the core. The fifth fundamental of leadership is managing change. "The pace of change has accelerated greatly. Leaders need to face and manage change in a constructive way and be adaptable, agile, and creative. Leading your team through change will ensure a successful change."[4] Our success came from leveraging leadership across our entire workforce. Leaders existed throughout our organization. They may not have had the titles to identify them as such: however, they were there, hiding in plain sight. As titled leaders, we needed to be open to new ways of working, new ways of engaging, and new ways of leading.

One of the biggest hurdles was teaching leaders how to manage with compassion and to coach compassionately. Managers often interpret these concepts as weakness or caving to the employee needs. In fact, "a coaching culture drives engagement, productivity, and accountability. Leaders who are trained as compassionate coaches inspire meaningful conversations to build relationships, create hopefulness, and bridge communication gaps. Winning teams always have a great and trusted coach."[5]

To help our partners learn how to coach with compassion, we identified three sub-categories: signs that a person is not demonstrating compassion, behaviors signalling compassion, and indications that compassion is being misunderstood.

NOT COMPASSIONATE

- No interest in asking questions about the person.
- Business is business.
- Uncomfortable discussing anything on an emotional level.

Behaviours Signalling Compassion

- Interested in other people not related to work.
- Shows empathy.
- Viewed by others as sincerely caring.

Compassion Misunderstood

- Let people off the hook to avoid conflict at all costs.
- Does not hold people accountable.
- Tries too hard to be compassionate and ends up being manipulated.

COACHING WITH COMPASSION COMES MORE EASILY TO SOME than others. Those who master this skill create a safe environment and high functioning teams. Their teams are committed, accountable, and focused on achieving results.

Ultimately all roads lead to the final of the seven fundamentals of leadership, achieving results. Leaders who inspire their team, provide purpose and show that it is possible to achieve amazing results and scale to new heights. Being creative, agile, and coming up with great strategies is great but execution surpasses everything.

While on our leadership adventure, we had some non-financial wins that solidified our position as leaders within the organization. The Health and Safety performance of our facility had been dismal. Our poor health and safety performance mirrored our negative culture. Under the new leadership team, health and safety was our platform for change. Our team created and implemented a Health and Safety Program that was based on the recognition of positive health and safety behaviors. Discipline was the last resort, not the first, except in the case of serious infractions. The program was adopted by our organization's facilities across the globe and established our facility as the benchmark for Health & Safety.

Earlier we talked about culture and the intrinsic value of leadership. We reviewed the value of time invested in gaining trust, communicating for transparency, earning respect, and building resiliency. The goal of this chapter has always been to validate that leadership has a direct impact on results. The actions of organizational leadership have the power to set the direction of the company. It gives me great pleasure to end on such a positive note. After years of consistent labour interruption during negotiations, the company, the leadership, the union, and the employees, turned a corner. There has been no labour interruption in more than 10 years.

I am honoured to have been part of this leadership team, a workforce of proud employees and partners with the union and community leaders. Although the adversity we faced may not be evident, our challenges were epic. The organization transformed, fostered a supportive team culture, and contributed to the community. As a leadership team, we were able to drive full speed ahead long enough to reach sustainability, celebrating our milestones along the way.

I began this story, this road trip, with my parents, my first example of great leadership. I have been fortunate to experience both good and bad examples of leadership in my career; those I wish to emulate, and those I choose to put aside but not forget. When I reflect on all my professional experiences,

I can affirm that they have all helped me to grow. As my esteemed colleague says, "growth comes from all directions".

I hope that some of my experiences will resonate with you. I hope that you find the motivation to AIM (align, inspire, measure) your teams. They are counting on you.

2
SURVIVING THE SHARKS IN SUITS

By Alexander L. Lutchin

The definition of a "corporate shark in a suit" used as a noun is ***a greedy, crafty person who takes advantage of others often through dishonesty, extortion and/or deceitful means***. In my experience they are very charming, often talk a lot and sound really smart, convincing people to trust them as they seem to have everything figured out. Corporations are filled with an array of personalities; most people have good intentions and are supportive. However, from time to time there will be someone around you who is not trustworthy, and it is good to understand how to recognize potential trouble and ways to cope with the situation for positive outcomes.

I have had my share of exposure to corporate sharks in my career and one thing I have learned: it is difficult to win with these people. It took me a long time and quite a bit of stress and pain along the way to get wise on how to recognize a shark early and find the best way to navigate around them. You can get eaten alive and they strike when you least expect.

I could never understand why another human being would want to hurt someone else. I was very naïve that everyone wanted to do good and be kind. I have learned this is not necessarily the way the corporate world works.

My name is Robert K.C. Smith. I am committed to integrity and hard work. Known for giving 110% of myself to the organizations I worked in, I exceeded goals and objectives continuously. I have always been a very strong and well-liked leader, a team player, and I constantly put the company at the front of the line in my life.

When I look back at my career I know now that I had blind spots; I did not spend enough time building relationships with people of influence in the organization. For example, I did not make it a priority to spend time at social and/or sporting events and I was not a great golfer, so I missed many opportunities to connect in casual but very meaningful ways. Most importantly I never understood how to navigate through the shark-infested hallways where people can get consumed by those with powerful hidden agendas and devious ways to make others look bad so they can look good. Sharks are sometimes hard to identify until it's too late. They can be exceptionally smooth: saying one thing to you, then turning on you the moment you are out of sight. I did not understand how to look for clues, follow the breadcrumbs, and identify important behaviours in order to intervene and better manage these potentially problematic people.

My first exposure to this type of personality occurred when I was working on developing a license application to start a new television station in Ontario. I was part of the core team who identified the opportunity and created a small group of professionals who came together to get the project moving. One of them was Bob who joined the team based on his ability to raise funds – our leader thought he would be a good fit. It turned out to be a nightmare.

Firstly, I was the one who found the deep-pocket investor to help with the financial piece and to attract others. However, guess who got the credit and the significant bonus for finding the deep pocket – Bob. It did not stop there; eventually over time, Bob actually attempted a coup of sorts to take over the project completely and leave the rest of us in the cold.

The lesson there for me was you have to fight harder for what is yours. I left myself vulnerable and sharks love vulnerability – they feed off it. The second lesson from this experience was that I needed to be much more aware of what was happening around me and follow my gut instincts.

The next exposure to one of these types took place while I was working in a senior organizational role and reporting to a Board. I was not a political person and thought that as long as I delivered and performed well, all would be good. Not the case. I soon realized that a handful of directors were constantly working behind my back and second guessing almost everything I did. When I look back on it now, I can see it was a very difficult and somewhat toxic environment. I eventually left the organization, but I should have left sooner. With sharks, the odds of winning are not favourable, so either you leave or get really good at managing them, which is stressful and not always worth the effort.

My next tour of duty took me to a high-profile group of companies. I inherited a dysfunctional team that was struggling, so my first goal was to get everyone working with each other and pulling together. I was still convinced that performance was more important than personality, so my focus was on achievements and making things work. I even took on more responsibility as needed. Everything was going very well. We were making great accomplishments heading towards success. However, the Board decided to hire a consultant to help get the organization moving forward at a faster pace.

Well, it turns out the consultant was the quintessential shark. Very smooth and articulate, the consultant presented as a team player, so it was very hard to see through this veneer. In essence, this person operated from hidden agendas and they were not good ones. Instead of coaching me and assisting, this leader actually began making friends with my direct reports and having private meetings with them. His ill intent completely blindsided me.

One day he actually held a meeting with my team, and I was not invited. I could see the writing on the wall, and the message was not positive. Within a couple of months, I was walked out on a Friday; the same happened to my boss a few months later. One of the few people left standing was, you guessed it, the shark who created the organized chaos. Sharks always take care of themselves.

Before I move on, I want to share one other example of dealing with these unscrupulous people. I had a business acquaintance, whom I will call Joe; he was outgoing and charismatic. You always felt that he was being supportive. He told me he had it in for another business acquaintance, and I observed him over time strategically orchestrate this person's "death by a thousand cuts". Little by little, he manipulated others into believing they were not good for the organization and were eventually squeezed out.

I watched this but still thought that we were friends until, as time went on, I realized I was also being undermined; the death by a thousand cuts was now aimed towards me. Joe worked from two agendas: his own and a broader agenda, making everyone think he cared about them. The hidden agenda was not always obvious, but it was often demonstrated in the way he created negative emotions and sowed uncertainty. Joe was crafty and manipulative and at times, he got his way at grave cost to others. People like Joe have selective feelings and are very calculating. What I learned from my experience with Joe was that I need to ask more questions, talk less, listen more and connect the dots early to get the real picture.

※

SO, NOW I WAS THINKING: "OK, I NEED TO DO SOME serious self reflection because clearly, I have blind spots that keep leaving me vulnerable and exposed to these deadly forces that walk the hallways". I needed to come to terms with myself that performance doesn't always save you, but performance and personality working together is much better. I was not all that good at making small talk and did not spend enough time building relationships with those around me, especially people of influence.

What I realized was that I was rarely around bosses who were self-aware or had a coaching leadership style – they were for the most part directive in nature and only cared about themselves and their agendas. From this perspective, I learned the importance of finding a mentor with influence in the organization who can be supportive, provide direction to circles of influence, and help burgeoning leaders create a strong visible executive presence. I wish someone had tapped me on my shoulder after the first shark attack to suggest this; however, I am not sure I would have listened. Things would have gone better for me if I had adopted this one simple and yet effective strategy.

I learned I needed to change my style of leadership and my executive presence. It was tough to admit, but it was the only way I could envision how to move forward and develop.

I did some research and concluded that a coaching leadership style was a great fit for me, even though it was something I had not previously considered. The reality was I was going to take a fresh approach and start with a clean slate, get rid of the baggage – jettison overboard, and move on, which is what I did. My journey of growth starts here.

All this reflection about developing a coaching leadership style reminded me of someone who was a wonderful coach for me, although I did not realize it at the time – my flying instructor. Reg had all the attributes of a great coach. He was focused, lived in the moment, was compassionate, had bounds of patience, was very engaged, a great listener, asked questions, and demonstrated trust and respect toward me. Of course, he demanded excellence on the flight deck and did so effectively without being overbearing.

On a beautiful Sunday morning in April, we had just touched down on runway 24, and Reg asked me to exit on Charlie taxiway and stop. I thought, "Really? This is odd."

Guess what happened next? He turned to me and said, "Robert, it's time for you to fly solo." Then he opened the door of the plane and left. That was it – he never looked back at me although I was hoping he would, so I could motion to him get back to the airplane.

There I was alone in the cockpit; the sun was dancing off the propeller liked diamonds, and I just sat there wondering what I should do. I needed to draw on my inner courage, strength and self awareness, and I needed to trust myself. I remember the tower calling me on the radio and wanting to know what my intention was. After what felt like an eternity of mulling this over in my mind, I called the tower and requested permission for takeoff. It was a feeling like none other when I roared down the runway, reached takeoff speed, and gently pulled back the wheel. I was airborne!

I will always remember that experience. Reg had more

confidence in me than I had in myself, and by showing this to me, he allowed me to have confidence in my own ability to take on the challenge and fly that plane. I wanted to become a compassionate and effective coach like Reg.

I was intent on changing my leadership style and wanted to learn more about my gaps, opportunities, and strengths. I had no idea what this was going to look like until one day, I attended the ICF Toronto Chapter annual conference and listened to a guest speaker from the Weatherhead School of Management, Case Western Reserve University in Cleveland. The professor discussed the differences between Positive Emotional Attractors – PEA – and Negative Emotional Attractors – NEA.

I recall wondering to myself, "What is this about?" I had never heard of this before. My first response was to leave the seminar and go for a coffee, but as the speaker continued, my attention was captured. He talked about the ways in which human beings interact with each other and why things do or don't happen, and how our minds can be either opened or closed towards change. It was a fascinating lecture! At the break, I introduced myself and asked how I could know more. Weatherhead offered a certificate coaching program, so I enrolled and spent the next year studying their amazing program.

In preparation for the program each student had to do a 360 feedback report that was called Emotional and Social Competency Inventory, administered by Korn Ferry. It provided great insights into how others saw me. Going through the program was highly rewarding, and we bonded as a class. We learned from each other, laughed, and cried a bit along the way as we dug deep into who we are through self-reflection.

The coaching model of leadership was different from anything I had learned up to this point in my life. I have often asked myself, where would I be now had I been exposed to this concept early in my career? The fundamental pillars of being a coach are many, but two stand out above the others: to be an active listener and ask thought-provoking, compassionate questions that lead to change and solve problems. Learning to stop talking and start listening was the hardest part of all of this – so simple, yet so difficult.

We were assigned into groups of three to practise our newfound art of coaching. These were hard sessions filled with emotion and intent that revealed the benefits and power of coaching as opposed to being a directive type of leader. Some of us are natural coaches – like my flight instructor. However, for people like me, this was a process I needed to learn, practise and practise some more.

The most valuable piece in all of this for me was understanding Emotional Intelligence (EI) and putting that into action. The thing about EI is that anyone can learn this if they have the passion and intention to do so. This will help in building stronger relationships and communicating effectively. Emotional competencies are as important as technical skills and are critical for anyone leading people. It takes hard work and focus but is well worth the effort – the positive outcomes are boundless. Building strong relationships with a circle of influencers is invaluable. Working with a coach and/or mentor is a key part of this learning as it will help create self-awareness from hearing their perspective on their observations as to what attracts sharks to you. Staying in a Positive Emotional Attractor mindset and helping others to do the same will set you apart and give you an advantage when dealing with sharks. Building meaningful relationships both vertically and horizontally is "mission critical" to staying ahead of the power curve. Doing so provides visibility on what is going on around you and provides important intelligence to help guide you. I learned the hard way that carving out the time to invest in relationship building is essential to a successful career path.

Sharks in suits are drawn to accolades, power, and control, and they need to have their egos fed. Sharks will isolate their targets using marginalization and manipulation, moving in for the kill once they smell blood in the water. My experience taught me to cautiously work with them and stay one step ahead. Choosing to fight with sharks is not recommended; their win-at-any-cost philosophy means they won't hesitate to use devious or malicious strategies. Winning for them may result in less than positive outcomes. That is why heightened self-awareness, assertiveness and self-confidence are vital to surviving in shark-infested waters.

Dealing with people who work from hidden agendas is not easy. They can pop up everywhere, even in volunteer organizations; however, they can be managed. The most important strategy is to recognize these people early in the process. Be mindful of behaviour patterns and trends and pay attention to the breadcrumbs they leave behind so you can build a picture and ask questions for deeper insight into their true intentions.

This brings me to my final thoughts around personality vs performance. Performance on its own sometimes will not save us from harm; sharks in suits are always looking for ways to create confusion and tension. They create distraction and then make their move. That is why personality plays a key role in survival. Building relationships that are engaging and meaningful provides a foil to the sharks – it makes the situation much more difficult for them to execute their mission of creating separation and division.

The school of hard knocks taught me to take time to build strong supportive relationships, to actively listen and learn about the people you work and associate with. Spend time socializing, networking, and building that all-important circle of influence; this will help prevent a shark attack or at least blunt it. If someone is out to do harm, you will have a buffer of influencers to support you.

I want to close our time together with these thoughts. There are more good people in the world than bad; we just have to seek them out and surround ourselves with like-minded colleagues and friends whom we can trust and respect. We also need to equip ourselves with powerful soft-skill tools by building our emotional inventory so we may achieve potential and success regardless of the situation.

What goes around comes around, and Karma is not kind to those who conduct bad deeds, so make sure you do not let sharks define you. As I move forward in my life, I find far more satisfaction with being grounded in the Positive Emotional Attractors than Negative Emotional Attractors. Adopting a coaching style of leadership and life in general has been very rewarding, and it has helped me to become the leader I am today. I know my value and I will always stand in my power.

Each of us has the capacity to be a great leader and make a lasting contribution to our company, community and family. The time to start is now – it is never too late to change and grow. Some folks may be born leaders, but for most of us, we learn the art of leadership through hard work, intentional learning, and a commitment to be our very best, which will allow us to achieve successes we never thought possible.

❧ 3 ☙
LEADING WITH EMPATHY:
BEING EMPATHETIC WHILE MAINTAINING YOUR AUTHENTICITY

By Aline Ayoub

The world we live in, work in, and lead in has changed dramatically in the last year. We are spending an increasing amount of time online 'alone', but we are more connected to one another now than ever before. In fact, with information becoming a commodity, and with consumers' reliability on e-commerce, the retail competitive landscape is dramatically shifting to a context in which meeting the customers where they shop has become the norm.

My name is Xavier French. It took me a while to recover from turning fifty years old. I vividly remember when my father turned fifty. He said *that it was time for celebration and acceptance*. My father was an optimistic man and getting older was not going to change his attitude. I felt there was still a lot I needed to accomplish, and that time was running out. I did not feel like celebrating or accepting. I felt like a ticking clock.

At the age of fifty-four, I am now a regional executive vice-president for an international retailer, with over fifteen years of experience in the retail industry. I define myself by my job and have struggled throughout my career with balancing family and work. I live with my three teenage daughters in the heart of Manhattan. Colleagues will speak about me for my ability of getting results and my worldwide recognition for the best sales achievement during three consecutive years. I am known for my loyalty to my employer and my adherence to its cultural norms and values.

It is not my fault!

I have been working for the world's largest retailer and have proudly delivered ten-digit sales increase year after year. I have built a worldwide stellar team of twelve sales professionals. My approach was to combine professionalism with effective interpersonal skills and persuasive communication abilities. My region was the envy of the company. I was poised for a successful future.

Unbeknownst to me, the world was hit by an unexpected pandemic, spearing a hard stop to what I thought was my most valuable asset: work. Such an unforeseeable predicament resulted in creating a chaotic chain of events which caused economic crashes, mass shutdowns, and unemployment skyrocketing to historic levels. Notwithstanding millions of people who have died from the virus worldwide.

My region retail stores experienced a decrease of seven percent in sales across the world. Thirteen percent of employees were laid-off and three stores experienced a complete shutdown as a result of the virus outbreak.

I have found myself at home with my three daughters startled by the unknown.

Nothing could have prepared me for this.

※

LOSING THE PATH

For the first time in my career, I felt fear, angst, and discomfort. I also lost my leadership bearings and felt inadequate to deal with this catastrophic event. My fall back plan was to rework the sales projections for the region. I couldn't bear the thought of not meeting the sales plans. I forecasted a ten per cent increase instead of the initial plan of fifteen per cent. That move went against my grain and made me feel nervous.

I knew I had to call a meeting with my team. I made a personally difficult decision to disclose a smaller sales increase. I concluded that talking about sales was the topic which defined our group synergy. Therefore, it was a conversation I could handle in spite of all the changes happening around me. In the quest of sounding 'in charge' albeit the growing uncertainty, I fell into the trap of telling instead of asking. I did not resist the urge to issue orders instead of describing the task or ask my team for their input. I was impatient and not supportive of my team, let alone asking how they were coping.

Three months later, I found myself still struggling with keeping my team together. I had to decline vacation requests and made them work overtime in order to keep up with the unexpected workload. They started to show signs of disengagement and sales continued to decline. It was clear I needed to change my approach. My role as leader became shattered. I needed more than a logical mind, strategic thinking, assertiveness, and power. The old paradigm which was focusing on getting results was no longer working.

I needed to pause and take a step back in order to carefully examine the needed changes in order to get different results. As Steven Coveys said in his book, *The Seven Habits of Highly Effective People*, "If you want to break the cycle, you need to carve out time to sharpen your saw"[1].

❦

THEODORE ROOSEVELT

Synchronicity made me come across Theodore Roosevelt's words: "Nobody cares how much you know until they know how much you care"[2]. How can that be? I always defined myself on what I knew and my job, but not on how much I cared!

This discovery was the beginning of a long journey in which I started to redefine my whole person: mind, body, and spirit. I needed to regain my confidence, re-examine my beliefs and my values, and create meaningful time with my daughters. I needed to reach out to a personification that represented a larger person than myself. It became clear that I could not continue to define my successful leadership by my results alone. There was a lot more needed in order to get back on track with my team and reappropriate the success we were known for.

What I needed to do was to transform into a new avatar: an avatar of a leader adapted to an ecosystem unlike anything I'd experienced before.

❦

THE CREATION OF MY BRAND-NEW AVATAR

Thinking that I needed to rewire my leadership style and admit it was no longer efficient, was agonizing. I knew I needed to re-engineer my playbook. The way I lead was no longer adequate to the changes that were unfolding before me. I needed to redirect my power differently.

While reviewing my notes on a course I attended on leadership, I came across the following: *"to attune yourself to your team's feelings, you must get in touch with your own emotions and understand how to express them"*. This note written in haste during that course turned out to be a revelation. My transformation started with an in-depth self-reflection. I needed to understand who I was, what my values were, and why I thought, felt, and acted the way I did. I went as far as asking myself how I could be a better father. I needed to understand what drove me in order to engage with the change.

Then I asked myself the following questions: What does my team need from me now? What keeps them up at night? Who knows what will work best? Should short term solutions take priority over long-term solutions? What are the new business challenges we are facing? Am I willing to take the risk of a wrong decision? Which resources are at my disposal? How will I instill trust with my team? How can I afford to allow them to take the vacation time they all felt they needed?

I decided to share my journey with my team, as well as my emotions and my challenges. I shared my values (even though they suddenly differed from those of the company) and declared that I would work through their fears, hopes and needs. I promised them that from now on, I would prioritize their innovative and adaptive skills over their abilities of achieving sales results. That was a major shift!

It took a while to instill credibility and shatter confusion. After all, it was a complete turnaround. Some people would also call it a disruption. I made sure I was consistent with my new self and as we were moving forward, my listening skills were also geared around their struggles which allowed me to intervene and helped them find solutions with their own teams. I found myself supporting my team without criticizing, judging, and regulating them. I was even able to support them with approving vacation they were longing for.

What sealed my transformation was the attestation of regaining my team's engagement and
witnessing their ability to grow and deliver results beyond self-imposed limitations.

Advocating my transformation

A year later, I am deeply engrained in my new leadership style, I can confidently say I belong to the category of empathetic leaders.

While I remain focused on adapting my business models to protect the financial health of the company, I consistently remind myself to consider the human.

I have found myself developing stronger connections, helping the team in replacing complexity of the disruption while working with clearer goals, and developing mechanisms replacing the ongoing fear of not being good enough, with a calm demeanor. Although the shift is more of a people-centric approach, I regained my self-confidence by paving the way and being assertive in my decision-making. I succeed in keeping the team on track, and yet remain being open and flexible to the ongoing changes.

Finally, I am achieving all this with compassion. I have definitely moved towards helping my team.

Since we need to constantly shift the way we do business, resiliency plays a big part in my success. Driving growth through creating clear processes is part of the past. To the contrary, I am more adaptable and responsive to change. I am responsive in a way that I can adapt to my team's needs, which are always changing. Consequently, we have been successful adjusting to our customers' behaviours.

I conducted a skills analysis of my team which allowed me to understand their strengths and weaknesses. The findings helped me better align the skills of my team members with the changes required in order to maintain our competitiveness. As a result, the efficiency of my team does not rely on any rigid processes, but on a hybrid workforce model in which their skills were used to benefit the whole team as much as to their own self. I focused on what made more sense moving on together and using a linear leadership approach in which skills were shared and utilized as needed by the business. Since our business was trending to be accessible online, where, and how the work was done was based on what made more sense to drive the engagement of my team.

I instilled a communication flow whereas my team was able to communicate freely, resulting in a broader exchange of new ideas, also creating space for them to support each other. Being open to discussion resulted in understanding my reports point of view, made my connections more authentic, and fostered my ability to influence them in getting results together as a team.

Moving Through Regaining Excellence

Do you understand exactly who your team is? Have you taken the time to figure out, what is a day in their life? What are their ambitions? What are their challenges? Only then can you build around that and make decisions based on accurate perspectives. Getting to know your team is the best way to lead towards the finest course of action for unilateral success, and the business as a whole.

I know I am making the right judgement call because I regained the courage to make difficult decisions using an empathetic approach at the forefront of all my decision-making. Having a window into their personal lives, results in finding ways to support them.

I embrace resiliency and admit I don't know-it-all. I treat failures as opportunities to grow future successes. I find my team is mirroring my behaviour and is more focused and productive through constant change and continue to thrive even when things are difficult. I welcome diverse perspectives and choose to respond positively to change and challenges.

I am being proactive in the face of ambiguity. I turn to my own values as anchors to reassure myself I am doing the right things for my team and the business. It is amazing how adhering to my values removed my anxiety and stress to a level that helps me continue to lead with empathy.

Empathy Can Be Learned

Stepping into another person's shoes becomes natural when you have lived through similar experiences. Thinking back, both my team and I were going through the same challenges. When I opened up to disclose my feelings and my plan going forward, we were able to find a common ground. The challenge was for me to gain trust, which I have accomplished by being transparent, consistent, and human.

The good news is that you can learn how to lead with empathy. It has to be regular and ongoing in order to be sustainable. Business priorities must be in the following order:

1. People
2. Customers
3. Growth
4. Shareholder value

Do you remember the time I had my priorities completely wrong? People were part of the equation; however, they were last in priority. The growth of the business was always first.

I nurtured and built a skill which has helped me become a better person, a better father, and a better leader. Building trust, empowering my team, tapping into their strengths have resulted in driving the business forward.

I understand my main responsibility is a human job. The influence I have on my team has grown since I started to understand them. They feel it and believe it. I manage to create a safe space promoting open discussions, establishing emotional connections, and nurturing resilience.

❧❧❧

TAKE AWAY

I have never thought of empathy as one of the most important qualities I needed to be an efficient leader. It is now apparent that being empathetic healed the dysfunctional team I was leading. It sealed our relationship and allowed me to freely express my anger and fears. While sharing my personal journey was uncomfortable, it shattered mistrust and confusion caused by many disruptions. It actually built trust and undoubtedly helped the team work better together.

I am happier at home and at work. Regaining self-confidence has a direct impact on acknowledging my competence. I am in control. Being in control allows me to make the right decisions. I measure my competence by my ability to create synergy in my team while meeting the sales targets. I reward my team for being innovative and being able to adapt to the retail competitive landscape.

People listen with their emotions. Emotion colours how they interpret facts and generates the energy to drive their actions. Understanding emotions, is listening without judgement, and making room for harnessing new ideas.

Making the information available to your team fosters transparency and help them understand the issues. To harness their skills in a way which will benefit all of them is extremely powerful, because in times of uncertainty and fear, it facilitates the flow of energy which feeds into each team member.

The power to harness leading with empathy derives from addressing four critical needs:

1. Challenge your belief and adjust your own perspectives.
2. Create a working environment of trust.
3. Put people first.
4. First, speak from the heart then from the head.

Following these steps will create a spiral of success.

To paraphrase Einstein, business leaders cannot fall victim to the insanity of doing the same thing over and over again and expecting different results. Agility and adaptability are leadership behaviours by which your success will stem from being open to complexity, change and ambiguity. Adaptability in the workplace is being flexible and having the ability to respond effectively to change. This willingness to learn continuously as a way of adapting to change in order to remain current, is a differentiator between successful and unsuccessful leaders. Being a true human leader means recognizing other employees as humans. It is being able to recognize their potential, ambition, feelings, and creative thinking.

Structuring my team in such a way that these human characteristics were brought out into the forefront, inspired, and amazed me. By being my whole self, they were able to do the same.

Today I spearhead the international operations of the

company and have built a team with whom I pursued with a people-centric approach, being a good listener and by simply being myself. This level of authenticity has bolstered better relationships, better decision-making, and has reinforced the most important part of my job – the people.

To truly be an effective leader, the starting point is self-awareness. Once you know how your own leadership style plays out at work, the possibilities for pondering its impacts on your team are endless. There are innumerable ways to effectively lead your team, and there are also many ways in which your team can overdeliver. Once you establish your leadership style and the working styles of everyone in your team, exceeding the expectations of the work ahead will be a natural occurrence.

By tapping into my employees' emotional needs, I was able to unleash their full potential which otherwise would have been limited by my rigid expectations and processes. They increasingly felt more inclined to take risks, which culminated into positive results in an ever-changing business climate, and a happier working environment. As a result, being progressive and innovative became characteristics I seek in my growing team. I regularly celebrate and encourage a steady flow of flourishing ideas which help our business move forward.

I am always challenging myself to become a better leader, a better father, and a better person. I consistently raise the bar on my aspirations and continue to transform from within, beginning with my mindset, values, and beliefs. My next challenge is to develop a deep understanding throughout the company of what is needed to drive value creation with our people and then combining it with a shared perspective of being able to deal with complexity, a changing retail landscape and the opportunities that lie ahead.

Be sure to center your decisions around humanity. Be a

leader that is a strategic thinker and an intuitive listener, strong yet nurturing, brave yet tolerant, empathetic yet authentic.

4
UNLEARNING LEARNED BEHAVIOUR

By Michele Bush

It was 2010 and we were still recovering from the global recession of 2008. At only 39 years old, I certainly was not the most seasoned executive, but I was confident that I had what was needed to take our company to the next level. Maybe too confident.

My idol had always been my Dad. He was a "finance guy" to the core. Like many who are in this profession, he started out in public accounting and auditing, holding leadership accountable for their spend and ensuring that they were compliant with government filings and tax obligations. Eventually, he progressed into a controllership function and has spent the last 10 years as the VP of Finance for a large international shipping company. I wanted to be the successful daughter who made him proud for following in his footsteps. We had endless conversations about business that just fascinated me. He'd tell me all about the financial drivers at his organization, the importance of profit margins and shareholder value. I paid close attention to his approach which, more often than not, involved cost cutting measures, reducing overhead and tightening the purse strings.

"Look after the pennies and the dollars will take care of themselves," was his favourite saying.

He was a no-nonsense guy who was able to move the company forward because he wasn't afraid to tell it like it is and he could mobilize his team to get things done, in what seemed like record time in some cases. I mimicked his style and leadership behaviours when I began my career in Accounting. It was learned behaviour from watching him for so many years and it was reinforced by observing the senior executives around me who had a similar mindset that financial results are the sole indicator of a company's success.

※

I WAS NEARING MY 40TH BIRTHDAY AND I HAD SOMETHING to prove. I had joined a logistics company as the Controller three years before and I took my direction from the CFO who had been with the company for almost 20 years. In business since 1960 and eventually expanding across all the Maritime provinces, the original owner did not have any children and when it came time to retire, he sold to a U.S. firm out of Boston that had its global headquarters in Europe. This had just happened prior to my arrival at ABC Inc. and my perspective of this decision, based on my father's influence as always, was that a buy out like this had meant only one thing - the opportunity to get better financial results. It was a chance to improve internal controls, find process efficiencies, enhance reporting systems and increase revenue per employee. However, the surrounding community had seen this quite differently. From their point of view this was a case of a well-established, family owned, local employer being swallowed up by a big conglomerate who was only in it for the money. Apparently, there had been quite a negative reaction at the time when this happened, but it was not on my radar.

Despite oversight from a global leadership team and US based counterparts supporting our business, the company was not growing organically like it had done in the past and the economic recovery was slower than expected. People were moving away from the East Coast in search of more prosperous job opportunities and the competition was starting to creep into our established customer base. The team in Boston decided to make some drastic changes in most of the businesses they owned, including ours, letting go three senior managers from the Canadian office. One of them was the CFO whom I had reported to and they immediately offered me a promotion to the role. Selfishly I saw this as an opportunity to advance my career, showing Boston and my father what I was made of and I didn't give much thought to the former employees who had given so much of themselves over the years.

My first major initiative was to lead the acquisition of a small inland transport company in Ontario. The global team had decided that an aggressive strategic growth plan was only going to be achieved through mergers and acquisitions and expansion of the business outside of the Maritimes. We were 300 employees at that point, and we were going to purchase XYZ Co. with a headcount of 100 people. Unbeknownst to me, this project had been in the works for months before I took over the CFO role. It was a surprise to say the least that the purchase agreement was already partially complete. This hit a nerve with me, and I got my back up. From day one of becoming the local lead on the project, I planned to demonstrate my financial acumen and show these executives that I could not only oversee this acquisition, but that I was going to make it even more cost effective than they had projected.

I immersed myself into this with everything that I had. Flying to Boston frequently, setting up afterhours calls with Europe so we could speak to our global staff in their own time zone, researching the competition in Ontario and recommending cost cutting measures to implement immediately upon the sale agreement being finalized. I was exhausted, but absolutely in my element and I was feeling more inspired than I had been in quite a while. The upcoming three-month deadline was not a deterrent for me, in fact it was exhilarating, until something unexpected happened.

It was a Friday night and the next day I would be turning 40. Although it was a milestone birthday, I hadn't given it much thought with the all-consuming M&A project taking up most of my energy. I was at the office a little later than usual and had phoned home to let my husband know that I wouldn't be much longer. He encouraged me to wrap it up for the night and come home as soon as I could.

My girls who were 12 and 14 at the time were hoping to have family movie night and spend some well-deserved time with Mom. I promised that I would be home in 30 minutes, but it was at least an hour later before I pulled into the driveway. As I opened the front door the crowd yelled, "SURPRISE!". I was so shocked, I just stood there. I must not have smiled or reacted with much appreciation because the sea of faces just looked at me as if they had done something wrong.

My girls ran up and hugged me unaware of the vibe that the guests had picked up on. My husband emerged and put his arm around me. He gently kissed me on the cheek and quietly whispered, "Snap out of it. Everyone is here for you!". He turned to the well wishers and smiled, doing his best to lift the mood by shouting "Let's get this party started!".

In the end it was a wonderful evening, filled with laughter

and dancing and a temporary break from the crazy hours that I had been keeping. The next morning as we were cleaning up, I apologized to my husband for being late. He admitted that maybe it wasn't the best idea to have a surprise party on a Friday night but that it was really hard to find time for anything since I was so wrapped up in this project.

"Oh, it hasn't been that bad!" I quickly dismissed him.

"Actually it has," he argued.

"I am out of excuses when the girls keep asking why Mommy looks so tired or has been at work so much and to be perfectly honest, it feels like you are turning into your father and I'm sorry to say this, but that's not a compliment."

I just stood there, silent, like I had been punched in the stomach. What came next was so unexpected to me. I didn't jump in to defend myself like I usually do when I feel slighted. To my disbelief I did not get offended or overreact. Instead, it was like a lightbulb came on making me realize that professional and personal, work and home, mental and physical, are not mutually exclusive.

I THOUGHT ABOUT WHAT THIS PROJECT WAS DOING TO ME and how negatively my family was being impacted by my involvement in it. I paused to reflect, thinking about our employees and those of XYZ Co., and the uncertainty that this acquisition would cause. I acknowledged that if we didn't take a step back and approach this differently, the outcomes would not be positive. After talking it through with my husband and saying it out loud so I could actually hear myself, I realized that up until this point the only things that I had been focused on were processes and profits and the looming deadline. I had not factored in the affects that a change of this magnitude would have on the people involved and their families, our customers and our reputation as a local employer. On Monday, things were going to change.

I contacted my Boston-based counterpart as soon as I got to the office on Monday morning. I explained to him that I had been doing some thinking over the weekend and that if this project was going to be successful in the long term we needed to go about it differently, starting with expanding the project team beyond the small group that it currently was. We set up a call with the European leads for 10:00 am so I could walk them through my idea. Initially both Boston and Europe shared their concerns about confidentiality, quite convinced that bringing too many additional players in at this sensitive stage could jeopardize the signing of the purchase agreement. They feared that making any changes to the project now would derail the timelines. I asked for a few uninterrupted moments to explain my position.

"Gentlemen, with all due respect, what made this company successful for over 50 years was the importance that the leadership placed on the employees, treating them with respect and trusting them. This business already experienced a significant adjustment when the ownership changed hands, and it impacted the employees and the perceptions of some of our once loyal client base. We may think that this project team as it stands has the knowledge to successfully achieve the expected outcomes of this acquisition, but I would argue that until we include some of the folks who know this local operation and the competition better than those of us who are in the room today, then we are not doing the project justice."

I paused for a moment and took a deep breath wondering what the reaction was going to be since this approach was quite a departure from how they had seen me behave for the last several weeks. To my pleasure, my Boston colleague thanked me for being honest and for sharing my opinion and said that they would be willing to consider it depending on what I was specifically proposing. So, I continued.

"You know that I am fully committed to the financial success of this company or else I would not have been placed in this role of CFO. In turn, I trust that your team did their due diligence in identifying that XYZ Co. is the best choice to help us reach our growth targets. At this stage, I would like you to grant me a 30-day reprieve.

"I will bring in our Operations Director, our HR Manager, seek out an employment law resource who knows the Ontario landscape, and a representative from our Accounting firm with a specialty in that province to ensure that we have covered all the bases; however, access to highly confidential information will be limited, in order to address your concerns. For example, only the HR Manager will be granted direct access to the proposed compensation packages of the management team of XYZ Co.

"Within one month, we will review the purchase agreement, identify any areas of concern or opportunity, develop a communications plan and modify any elements of the project plan that may need adjusting. This will all be done with the intention that it does not drag out the process, but rather it will ensure that people, productivity, profits and our employer brand are all considered equally so we achieve success in the long run."

By 5:00 pm that same evening, my recommendation had been approved. By Noon the next day, the newest members of the project team had signed the global "secrecy" agreement, they had been introduced to the contacts at XYZ Co., and they were up to speed on the status of the project. I gave them 24 hours to review the project plan and the draft purchase agreement and come prepared to share their high-level feedback, identifying any and all areas where they saw gaps or had significant concerns/questions.

What came back was exactly what I had anticipated – our new project members saw things that we had not. As an example, the HR Manager knew our benefits plan inside and out and even though there was already a defined step in the project timeline to merge the XYZ Co. employees into our plan, she conducted a side by side comparison of the coverage, flagging the minor and significant differences and she anticipated the concerns that these employees would invariably have.

The Operations VP identified a concern in the proposed reporting structure and recommended the management team at XYZ Co. report into the Canadian office instead of Boston which would improve communications. He also identified that the Health and Safety policies of XYZ Co. were not as stringent as our company and he highlighted an implied assumption in the project timeline that these practices of a higher standard at our company were to be adopted by XYZ Co. from day one. He challenged this notion and outlined the need for giving reasonable time for training and adoption to ensure a genuine change in behaviours.

They both commented on the lack of detail in the communication plan. They felt that sharing the news of the acquisition in the form of a general announcement to all employees at once was not ideal. They proposed that we involve roles like the Payroll Specialist, our IT Manager and some operational front line supervisors as soon as the deal was finalized so that they could be included on the communication team to address employee concerns; after all, these colleagues were already trusted and would be key to the success.

In the 30 days that the Canadian project team had been given, we were determined to demonstrate how factoring in the people aspects of our business decisions would have a direct correlation to the outcome of this significant endeavour, not only for XYZ Co., but for our existing employees too. We created a rubric with the major milestones of the project and listed 5 factors to consider for each proposed step.

We used this format to point out and recommend ways to address the fact that it wasn't only about WHAT had to be done to get this purchase agreement finalized and implemented, but also HOW this should be approached. The 5 factors we used for our "people impact" check and balance were Employee Experience, Productivity, Safety, Employer Reputation and Customer Relations. We asked ourselves how the announcement, the organization structure, the health and safety policy amalgamation and other aspects of the merger would affect these five factors.

❦

THE BIGGEST AHA! MOMENT FOR ME PERSONALLY IN ALL OF this was that I had been able to re-frame my thinking. I, like many leaders, focused primarily on making business decisions from the perspective of process and profit and end results. I had believed that if the decision was good for the business, then employee engagement would follow, but what I realized is it is actually the reverse.

When we take the time to consider the people aspects upfront, then the success will follow. By instilling this leadership mindset, we can leverage the triggers that inspire, inform, and motivate versus the unintentional consequences (of anxiety, mistrust, safety risk, lower productivity, and employee turnover), which are more likely to happen when we only put profits first. As leaders and role models, we need to be keenly aware that how we show up and how we behave directly affects the business results.

For this acquisition to be successful, we proactively anticipated impacts on all stakeholders and operational functions, ensuring that we put employees at the top of this key stakeholders list. In the immediate our new, altered methodology led us to more transparent communication and the development of Q&A sessions for XYZ Co., as well as our staff at ABC Inc. We made recommendations to invest in things like training and development and system improvements instead of my initial, narrowminded focus on cost cutting measures, and I am so proud to say that we were able to meet the sale agreement and transition date deadlines.

In the long term this has changed the way our leadership team approaches strategic initiatives. We have aligned our actions to our vision and values, and we have a more balanced perspective of the people and financial considerations of our decisions. Post acquisition, all of our supervisors participated in a comprehensive leadership development program which helped them to see that the biggest overhead cost – the employees – is what leads the company to increased productivity when they are more engaged and efficient.

Our Five-factor rubric became a standard process tool that is still used formally for some projects and informally for others, creating a habit-forming way of thinking. Of course, we must have a focus on the bottom line and ensure that we are as efficient as we can be, but we always look at the people impact as a key business driver.

How do we know that this is working? We have low turnover. There is healthy competition between the sites, which leads to process improvements and operational synergies. We have reduced the fill-time for staff vacancies, and we have been acknowledged as an employer of choice in the communities we represent.

My advice to other leaders stems from my personal experience of learning to let go of my tunnel vision and linear thinking. I invite and encourage you to open your mind to the notion that strategic business decisions must intentionally include the people factors at all stages. When we do this, the result is increased productivity and profits and an improved image of the employer brand.

※

FROM A BUSINESS PERSPECTIVE, I AM PLEASED THAT THIS leadership approach has become the norm at our company and continues to be recognized by the international management team. But even more importantly from a personal standpoint, I am looking forward to having my daughters watch me, learn from my behaviours, and follow in the footsteps of a successful female executive who can drive the company forward because of her tenacity and financial acumen, combined with her genuine desire to ensure the people factors are considered and employees are respected in every business decision, **always**.

5

THE EMOTIONALLY AWARE LEADER

By Wendy Woods

I arrive at my local coffeeshop, Susie Q's, at 6am. The barista hands me my latte and says with a smile "Thanks Jillian. Great to see you so early." After taking a sip, I sit down at a table – a rare luxury in my role as Director of Sales of Cali, a SaaS based web hosting service. I want to reflect on my last nine months at the company as I have had little time to do that since joining.

I joined with a mandate of doubling sales in the next two years. Not an easy feat but after growing the sales 2x at my previous tech company, I figured that my grit, work ethic, and strong market demand would make it an achievable goal. We were on pace for the year until Q3 and now it looks like we will miss the quarterly target putting our annual goal at risk. Based on what is currently in the pipeline, it will be difficult to meet Q3 unless something changes dramatically. I am under pressure from the Senior Leadership Team, as future funding depends on meeting these goals.

It's challenging to determine what's wrong given the

significant changes I made in my first three months. I exited two non-performers, moved in a top producer from my previous company, and hired Pam, the Chief Marketing Officer's niece. Additionally, I implemented daily stand-up meetings at 10 AM to review the pipeline, potential opportunities, challenges, and identify any support required. This worked well at my former company; it helped us zero in on problems and pivot where needed. Here, it doesn't seem to be working because when I challenge the team on their pipeline and prospects, several of them do not have a clear handle on things. Their lack of accountability and inability to troubleshoot is concerning. I don't think they understand the pressure we are under.

To address this, I improved the sales reporting to identify challenges much earlier in the process. I implemented more frequent one on one meetings with my team. These meetings focus solely on the obstacles they are facing with prospects, internal problems with other departments, or software challenges. This way, I can offer immediate solutions and guidance and run interference internally. I think the team appreciates having more of my time, attention, and expertise. Yet, the energy and enthusiasm that I had seen at Cali in the past, which indicates more collaboration and completion of sales, appear to be lacking. In fact, the team has been quite abrasive towards each other and even me. Something isn't quite right, but I just can't put my finger on it.

In addition to meeting the sales target this year, my other goal is carving out my strategic plan to ensure we meet our targets for next year, too. I have been working twelve-hour days and most weekends. Everything in my life has taken a back seat including workouts. My stress is high, but I am determined to achieve that sales target. I have been under more stress in previous jobs; I can easily manage it until year end, and I have a few days of vacation planned. Plus, I am driven by the bonus and promotion to Senior VP that comes with meeting that milestone.

I check my email before taking my last sip of my latte and preparing to leave. I find an unusual request from the CMO, Terence, inviting me for a late lunch today. I don't usually take lunch, and I am a little suspicious but of course, I agree.

Once we finish with the small talk and niceties, Terence gets to the point. "We had a family gathering last weekend where I had a chance to catch up with my niece Pam. I asked how she was finding her job and being part of your team." He grimaces as though he is uncomfortable and takes a long sip of water. "I think she might have had a few too many glasses of wine and she shared more than I expected. I thought you should know what she said."

In a classic demonstration of his caring leadership style, he asks, "Are you open to hearing it? My only motivation is ensuring your success."

I have heard other senior leaders at Cali talk about how Terence had mentored them and the difference it made in their leadership and career. Putting my ego aside, I realize that I need that too.

He begins by saying, "What Pam told me is shared by the entire sales team. They feel like you are constantly angry with them. They can always tell because your face turns bright red. At that point, they become intimidated and fearful that you might really lose it. They then acquiesce and agree, too afraid to mention their ideas."

I take a deep breath. *Really?* I think to myself, *my face goes red and yet no one had ever told me this.*

"Please continue," I request.

"In fact, Pam mentioned that in a few of your one-on-one meetings, you had emotional outbursts, leaving the staff feeling inadequate and angry. When they tried to explain or get some support, you didn't listen but became even more directive and demanding."

❦

I ASK TERENCE TO GIVE ME A MINUTE TO PROCESS AND reflect on my meetings.

I actually thought that I was just being focused on the end goal, giving them my best advice and trying to get them onside and motivated. Clearly my intentions had a different impact. While it is hard to hear, I know honest feedback like this is rare and an essential part of becoming a stronger leader.

"Go on," I encourage him. "Something tells me there is more."

"Yes there is. Apparently, most of the team is feeling disengaged and dissatisfied and starting to look for roles elsewhere. In fact, Marc, your top rep, is about to get an offer at a growing start-up known for poaching candidates".

That statement takes my breath away. Without Marc we are never going to reach our targets. He is not only a strong salesperson, but he is also a motivating force for the rest of the team. If Marc leaves, it will be like sinking a ship. I'm blindsided, yet I know I need to act quickly to prevent this loss.

"This is really hard to hear Terence. I appreciate your honesty and taking the time to give me much-needed feedback. What else?"

Terrence muses, "I can see you are a driven leader with strong technical sales skills and experience. However, understanding and managing emotions and those of others is not something we learned growing up or in school. My sense is that you may need some help in the more emotional aspects of leadership. Basically, I am talking about Emotional Intelligence (EQ) which in simple terms is knowing how you feel, how others feel, and knowing how to manage emotions."

"Terence, I'm confused. Emotions?" "I thought that too, but I learned a lot from my coach. Emotions tell us how we feel about the world and when we are feeling threatened or rewarded by a person or situation. Neuroscience can shed further light. Our brains are constantly scanning our environment for threats and rewards. When a threat is encountered the brain usually responds with the fight, flight, or freeze response, which is our body's natural response to danger.

The part of the brain responsible for detecting threats and for triggering this reaction is the amygdala, housed in the limbic system or the emotional part of the brain. While this area of our brains developed to keep us safe from physical threats like man-eating tigers, today it can also be activated by psychological threats. Receiving an angry email, your boss saying, "we need to talk", or being left out of an important meeting can all activate that response.

"The amygdala is so quick at receiving information, your emotions respond even before you are consciously aware of it. Think about when you get cut off in traffic. You may end up honking your horn, swearing, or shouting even before you realize what you're doing. That is how quickly the fight, flight or freeze response can take hold."

"You haven't even seen me drive" I quipped with an embarrassed chuckle. "Terence, what I do in the car is different from how I react at work."

"True," Terrence counters, "your reactions depend on the strength of the trigger. However, like being in the car, you may not even be aware of how quickly your emotions take over or how your reaction is interpreted by others. Your staff are definitely seeing and experiencing something that you are not even aware of."

I reluctantly admitted that he might be right. I have often

wondered about what my team's quizzical expressions meant when I was speaking to them. Clearly something was wrong. I asked Terence to tell me more.

"Another part of the brain that's important here is the Prefrontal Cortex (PFC) – located right behind the forehead. It's responsible for planning, decision making, problem solving, attention, managing impulses, and expressing feelings. It's also known as the Executive Function. Basically without the PFC, you couldn't do your job. When your amygdala gets triggered, it hijacks the PFC. You become less effective at all the PFC functions as your brain's and body's resources are redirected to manage the threat.

Have you ever noticed how it's so much harder to think when a co-worker has angrily disagreed with you, or when you feel upstaged at a meeting? That's your amygdala taking over and affecting your executive functioning."

Terence continues, "The good news is that developing your Emotional Quotient can help you recognize your emotions and develop strategies to bring your PFC back online by inhibiting the amygdala's signals. EQ can be learned *and* developed. As a leader it's critical to cultivate. According to Daniel Goleman, EQ expert, 85% of leadership competencies are in the EQ domain[1]"

I realize EQ is not as soft as it sounds, and it is clearly an area I need to develop. I muse aloud that Terence will tell me know how to do that.

He laughs. "I sure am. Think of this as an investment in your leadership. I have worked with Sloane, an International Coaching Federation certified coach, specializing in Emotional Intelligence, and I've seen a huge difference in my leadership, my team's level of engagement, and our results. I've already contacted her as she is exceptionally busy, and you don't have time to waste given your targets. She said if you reach out to her today, she will send you a link to complete the EQ-i 2.0 Leadership Report. She can meet this weekend to debrief you. From there, you can decide how often you want to meet. I've arranged for cost of the assessment and 6 months of coaching to be covered by your professional development allowance. You can dive right in."

Laughing, I comment, "I can see why your nickname is the Roadrunner: you move fast! I am grateful for your support and guidance. Once I begin this work, may we continue to connect?"

Patting my hand, Terence smiles. "Absolutely. I am here to support you."

※

By evening, I have reached out to Sloane, filled out the EQ-i 2.0 Leadership assessment and booked my debriefing appointment for 10 a.m. on Saturday.

As I head to her office, I'm nervous. What will the assessment reveal about me and my leadership? Can I make the changes in time to positively impact my team?

Immediately Sloane puts me at ease with her down-to-earth style and easy laugh. She explains that my assessment results and our conversation are confidential, and our focus is on my leadership development. She explains that we will walk through the report together. The report will indicate areas where I am excelling and will show how to leverage them further. It will also identify areas of growth so that I could improve those skills to further benefit my team and the organization.

"Jillian, thanks for sharing details in our previous conversation. I'm sure it hasn't been easy to see what's happening with your team, the issues and as well as what Terence shared with you. I am going to do our session a little differently than I would normally since time is of the essence. I'd like to zero in on key areas that, my experience has taught me will yield the greatest results." I could feel my shoulders start to relax.

"While you often hear people describing someone as emotionally intelligent or not, it's not that black and white. As you will see, there are many different competencies making up Emotional Intelligence. Most of us have areas that are strong as well as those that need to be developed. I will share the overall EQ score with you, but keep in mind that it's more of an indicator because this is an assessment tool, not a test where a high score is good and a low score bad. Plus, it's looking at the underlying competencies, in combination with what's happening at work, that can help us identify what's contributing to your success and what could be derailing it."

"It will help if I walk you through the EQ-i 2.0 Model of Emotional Intelligence. At the center of the diagram is your overall Emotional Intelligence which is comprised of five composites: self-perception, self-expression, interpersonal, decision making, and stress management. These are further broken down into 3 competencies for a total of fifteen. On the outer ring you can see that based on how you are using and balancing your EQ competencies, it could improve your well being, leadership performance and interpersonal relationships."

"Let's look at how the EQ-i 2.0 Workplace Report is different from the EQ-i 2.0 Leadership Report that I gave you. In the former, your EQ is a standardized score compared to a representative sample of the North American population. With the leadership one, you get the same standardized score, and you are also compared to the top 50% of leaders who took this assessment. These leaders scored 14 points higher than the general population and are represented by a gold bar above each score.

"Jillian, you will find this helpful as you can quickly see

how you are doing compared to high performing leaders. Ready to look at your assessment?" I nodded.

Sloane continued. "If we look at your overall EQ, we can see you are above average and considered in the mid range. Your overall score falls slightly below the gold bar and out of the leadership area. This tells us that there are probably some underlying competencies that could be improved so you can be a more effective leader. What would you like to focus on as we go through the report?"

I considered her question for a moment. "I'd like to know how to best leverage my efforts so I can start seeing immediate benefits."

"Ok," Sloane replies. "Let's focus on what I think could be most helpful today. In future sessions, we can dive deeper into the rest of the report."

"One area that may be holding you back is showing up as your lowest competency on the assessment; that is Emotional Self-Awareness or ESA. This is the foundation upon which the other fourteen competencies are built. Without ESA, it will be hard to boost your EQ. My experience tells me that with some improvement in this area you could start seeing positive results quickly. Should I continue?"

Nodding my head, I asserted my trust in Sloane and asked her to continue.

"ESA is about recognizing and understanding your own emotions, which includes being able to identify their subtleties, understanding their cause, and their impact on your thoughts and actions and those of others. Being more emotionally aware will help you see what emotions are arising, what produced them, and how they are affecting you and others at work. This is the first step to managing your emotions, so they don't negatively affect your team. Korn Ferry found that among "leaders with multiple strengths in emotional self-awareness, 92% had teams had high energy and high performance.² We'll address more of this in future sessions. Does that make sense?"

I nodded. "A friend mentioned something about a leader's emotions 'spreading'. Can you help me understand that?" I asked.

"Yes," Sloane Shared. "That's another reason to support the work we're doing. Emotional Contagion occurs when one person's emotions spread throughout a group and trigger similar emotions in others. This is especially true for leaders. Sigal Barsade found if a leader was in a negative mood, team members adopted that mood, and their performance suffered. The opposite was true of a positive mood where performance improved.³

Sloane asked me to describe a recent event where it would have been helpful to be more in touch with my feelings.

"A few weeks ago, I redistributed some accounts among the staff to improve the pipeline and boost sales with minimal impact on year-end bonuses. In my one-on-one meeting with Marc, he kept pushing me to return one of his accounts. I was mildly upset by his reaction, but I thought I was remaining calm. He said, 'Stop yelling, I am right here. You're getting angry because I don't agree with you. I've managed a team before, and I never would have undermined them like you did.' He slammed my office door shut. That evening, I realized my jaw was still clenched and my stomach was in knots. I understood that I was angry and defensive but hadn't connected with this in the meeting. My lack of awareness ended up stressing me out all day and put Marc in an uncomfortable situation."

Sloane asks what I'd like to happen in the future. I reply that I want the ability to identify my emotions in the moment. Just describing that one scenario shows how that would help me better manage conflict situations.

"What would be helpful moving forward?" she asks.

"I'd like a proven method I can incorporate on a daily basis." I reply.

Sloane suggests, "According to Goleman, mindfulness meditation is an effective way to develop self-awareness.[4] Companies like Google, Aetna and General Mills offer mindfulness programs. These programs help improve awareness in leaders and address other challenges like attention, stress, communication, and collaboration. Jillian, the power of mindfulness is also backed by scientific research. One study found that mindfulness meditation enhances the part of the brain associated with self-awareness.[5] Other research discovered a decrease in amygdala activity after mindfulness training.[6] With less activity in the amygdala, there is less impact on your PFC so you can recognize and better express emotions. You might think meditation is all about clearing your mind of all thoughts, but it's not. The mind actually wanders 46.9% of the time.[7] It's actually about 'the awareness that arises through paying attention, on purpose, in the present moment, non-judgmentally' according to Jon Kabat-Zinn[8]. Essentially, it improves awareness and makes us more present to what's happening within and outside us. Mindfulness gives you the space to choose. It's like that famous Viktor Frankl quote, 'Between stimulus and response there is space. In that space is the power to choose our response'[9]. What commitment would be helpful for you?"

"I've always wanted to start a regular mindfulness practice. I think I could do 20 minutes a day but feel like I would need to start with a guided meditation. Can you suggest one?" I asked, excited.

"Try Jon Kabat Zinn's 20-minute sitting meditation[10]. What could help support you in making and maintaining this commitment?"

I reply, "I could wake up twenty minutes earlier. Second, at times when doing it feels hard or inconvenient, I can remember that developing my ESA will help my leadership, my team, and the organization."

Sloane asks, "Is there a picture, quote, or token that could support that perspective shift?"

"Yes, I have a picture of our team taken at our annual conference, so I'll put it on my desk."

It occurs to me that I will need an accountability partner. I mention to Sloane that I will check in with Terence daily. I ask Sloane if she has any other tips for me.

"Another technique you could add to your day is called STOP. S stands for stop what you are doing for a minute. T is for take a few deep breaths and notice as it comes in and out of your nose. O is to observe your thoughts, feelings, and body sensations. See what thoughts are present. What emotions do you notice? How does your body feel? Tune in and be with whatever comes up. Research shows that simply labeling your emotions can make them less intense.[11] Finally P is, proceed with something that will support you in the moment, like grabbing a tea, asking for a moment to think, or taking a break. Find one or two times a day to STOP. It may prove helpful to use in challenging situations like meetings. Check in at the beginning, middle, and end of them. After stopping and taking a few breaths, notice the pain in your back, or anything else; the emotions that emerge like frustration, and any thoughts such as 'why aren't they listening to me'. To help you refocus on the meeting, proceed with what's helpful like being curious about their intentions or needs."

I agree that it would be helpful to have a tool to use throughout the day as my internal state shifts and changes. I inform Sloane that I will also ask one of my sales managers for feedback after every meeting about his perception of my emotional control.

Sloane smiles approvingly. We agree to meet the following

Saturday at the same time. I promise to email her if I face any challenges I cannot address on my own.

She suggests that our sessions over the coming months will allow us to explore the rest of the EQ-i 2.0 Leadership Report to see what else could be helpful for boosting my leadership style. I thank Sloane and leave eager to practice mindfulness and STOP.

ON MONDAY, I MANAGE TO GRAB A FEW MINUTES WITH Terence. "I didn't realize how important it is to be aware of my emotions. The EQ-i 2.0 leadership report, and Sloane, highlighted my low emotional self-awareness. Since it is the basis for developing the rest of my EQ, I have begun using two activities to build that awareness. She will coach me in the other EQ areas in upcoming sessions. Terence, will you be my accountability partner to ensure I stay on track with these activities?"

Terence nods. "You're doing the right thing, Jillian. I'm proud of you."

Effusing with gratitude, I thank Terence again for his honest feedback and for connecting me with Sloane. With their support and coaching, I know that I am on my way to becoming an emotionally intelligent leader.

LEADERSHIP AIM

EQ-i 2.0 Model of Emotional Intelligence

SELF-PERCEPTION

Self-Regard is respecting oneself while understanding and accepting one's strengths and weaknesses. Self-Regard is often associated with feelings of inner strength and self-confidence.

Self-Actualization is the willingness to persistently try to improve oneself and engage in the pursuit of personally relevant and meaningful objectives that lead to a rich and enjoyable life.

Emotional Self-Awareness includes recognizing and understanding one's own emotions. This includes the ability to differentiate between subtleties in one's own emotions while understanding the cause of these emotions and the impact they have on one's own thoughts and actions and those of others.

STRESS MANAGEMENT

Flexibility is adapting emotions, thoughts and behaviors to unfamiliar, unpredictable, and dynamic circumstances or ideas.

Stress Tolerance involves coping with stressful or difficult situations and believing that one can manage or influence situations in a positive manner.

Optimism is an indicator of one's positive attitude and outlook on life. It involves remaining hopeful and resilient, despite occasional setbacks.

SELF-EXPRESSION

Emotional Expression is openly expressing one's feelings verbally and non-verbally.

Assertiveness involves communicating feelings, beliefs and thoughts openly, and defending personal rights and values in a socially acceptable, non-offensive, and non-destructive manner.

Independence is the ability to be self directed and free from emotional dependency on others. Decision-making, planning, and daily tasks are completed autonomously.

DECISION MAKING

Problem Solving is the ability to find solutions to problems in situations where emotions are involved. Problem solving includes the ability to understand how emotions impact decision making.

Reality Testing is the capacity to remain objective by seeing things as they really are. This capacity involves recognizing when emotions or personal bias can cause one to be less objective.

Impulse Control is the ability to resist or delay an impulse, drive or temptation to act and involves avoiding rash behaviors and decision making.

INTERPERSONAL

Interpersonal Relationships refers to the skill of developing and maintaining mutually satisfying relationships that are characterized by trust and compassion.

Empathy is recognizing, understanding, and appreciating how other people feel. Empathy involves being able to articulate your understanding of another's perspective and behaving in a way that respects others' feelings.

Social Responsibility is willingly contributing to society, to one's social groups, and generally to the welfare of others. Social Responsibility involves acting responsibly, having social consciousness, and showing concern for the greater community.

Based on the Bar-On EQ-i model by Reuven Bar-On, copyright 1997
Copyright © 2011 Multi-Health Systems Inc. All rights reserved.
21500416201120

6

LOVING LEADERSHIP

By Julie A. Christiansen

As the Executive Director of a major not for profit, I had a truckload of responsibility. The government funded our operation, and in return we were expected to meet their quotas for client engagement, positive client outcomes, and follow-ups to document long-term success. I had always accomplished this goal by holding weekly meetings with my team, performing careful supervision to ensure they were on track to meet the government requirements, and troubleshooting any challenges in "making our numbers". The problem was, with a global pandemic shaping the way we worked, I could no longer hold those weekly meetings. Everyone was working in a bubble of their own, and I couldn't control the workflow the way I was accustomed to. Stressed, frustrated, and out of my depth in a virtual workplace, I was floundering.

I was burning out. I could feel it. I knew the symptoms well; this wasn't my first rodeo. Over the last 20 years in my various roles in human services, I've crashed and burned at least four times. So, I knew that this feeling of low-grade vibration in my body was anxiety. I recognized the other symptoms. The craving for more salty and sweet foods. My over consumption of coffee. Drastic weight gain. Brain fog. And the overwhelming need to control everything. Yup. Definitely burning out.

So, when my good friend invited me to take a long weekend for myself to enjoy some white water rafting, I jumped at the chance to exchange the stressors of my daily life for a little fun and adventure. On the way to the venue, my friend quizzed me about what had me so down. I filled her in on my challenge of trying to control all the moving parts of the organization while attempting to navigate uncharted territory as far as virtual services was concerned. I explained that even before the pandemic, staff was stressed. I had seen an uptick in absenteeism and higher consumption of extended health benefits. If people weren't calling out for sick days, when they did show up to work productivity was good, but it wasn't great. Once we had to make the shift to virtual services, I felt like things were even further out of my control. There was no way to ensure that people were actually doing their jobs.

"Sounds to me like you've got a few challenges, rather than just one," she remarked thoughtfully. "First of all, your management style is not only making you sick, but it may be contributing to the stress of your team. Second, all the rapid changes you have experienced this year seems to have produced a severe case of 'Future Shock' for you and your staff members. Third, you seem to be more focused on your need for control instead of the needs of the team."

"What exactly is Future Shock?" I asked her. She explained that it was a term coined by futurist Alvin Toffler, who described it as the negative effects of experiencing too much change with too little time to adjust. She said that the effects of future shock include something called hurry sickness and it featured anxiety, dehydration, headaches, stress-related illness, depression, absenteeism, presenteeism, and a host of other health challenges.

"Seems like both you and your team are suffering these effects. That's why you've got people calling in sick, and when they do show up, they're stuck in 'analysis paralysis' – too focused on trying to cope when they should be completing work-related tasks."

I must admit, I did not take kindly to her observation. But then she added, "Look. The success of the not-for-profit doesn't depend on how much you control things; it depends on the team's performance."

"Right." I agreed. "But they won't perform unless I carefully direct all of their activity."

She laughed out loud. "I'll tell you what," she offered. "When we get to the retreat, I'll introduce you to our guide for the weekend. Pay close attention to how he directs the trip downriver, and we'll compare it to your leadership style and see what we can learn."

Honestly, at this point I had no clue what she was talking about, but I figured I had nothing to lose by trying out her suggestion. So, I agreed to her challenge.

WHEN WE ARRIVED AT THE RETREAT, MY FRIEND practically launched herself out of the car and into the arms of a man whom I assumed was our guide. After a quick exchange of hellos, she introduced him to me.

"Tom, this is my friend I told you about. We're looking

forward to some adventure this weekend, and we're really eager to hear your insights about leadership too."

Tom took my hand in his for a hearty shake. "Nice to meet you! Welcome to my humble retreat. This weekend promises to be full of fun and excitement, risk and reward, daring and danger. Are you up for it?"

Tom's unbridled enthusiasm was contagious. "Sure!" I exclaimed. "As long as you can ensure that we'll survive the weekend, I'm in."

"You'll more than survive," he chuckled. "You'll walk away from this weekend a brand new person."

A brand new person. I liked the sound of that.

※

THAT EVENING, AFTER A HEARTY SUPPER, TOM SAT DOWN with me, my friend, and the others who had arrived at the retreat for a weekend of white water rafting.

"I need to ensure that you're equipped with everything you need to make this weekend fun and successful," he said. "I'll be sharing some of the key rules of white water rafting tonight, and before we ever set foot in a raft, I need to be certain that you all understand the rules, you know what the rafting instructions mean, and how to execute them. There will be no time to ask questions as we whip through white water, so now is the time to ensure you understand everything."

We all nodded in agreement.

He then said something that tilted my world on its axis. "For the next two days, I am your leader. But as your leader, I cannot just TELL you what to do. If that is all I do, this adventure will fail; worse, it could prove fatal to some or all of us. My job is to work ALONGSIDE you. To coach you and to guide you through the rapids so that we not only emerge on the other side safely, but we have fun doing it."

Looking over at my friend, I could see her smiling and nodding. She caught my eye and winked. Tom continued, "No one gets into a raft without the proper PFD. You must be prepared to fall overboard, even while you're doing everything to prevent that from happening; that is why a personal floatation device is non-negotiable. We want you to stay in the boat, and some of the instructions I share tomorrow morning will be to make sure that happens."

"One of the most important things to remember," Tom cautioned, "is that you must always keep your eyes on the OBJECTIVE. Do not, I repeat, do not get distracted by whirlpools or boulders sticking out of the rapids. Always keep your gaze downriver. If you focus on the obstructions to our passage through the rapids, you will end up steering us into those obstructions. Keep your eyes on the end goal."

"Next," he ventured, "is the survival plan. We must come prepared for whatever the river might throw at us, and the survival plan needs to be in place BEFORE we get in the raft. As I said before, there will be no time to negotiate a good plan to manage contingencies once we are in the water. We will go over the survival plan tonight and tomorrow so everyone is on board. It is absolutely essential that you listen carefully and respond immediately to the instructions as they are called out. The survival of the team depends on it."

I looked over at my friend, crossed my arms, and nodded smugly. I knew she was hoping I would see the parallels between Tom's approach to guiding us on the river to my philosophy on management. *You see,* I thought self-righteously, *I do need to be giving specific instructions to the team. They won't survive without me.*

But then Tom threw me off kilter again when he said, "Remember, everyone. I won't be sitting in the back of the raft eating bon bons and tossing out instructions here and there. I'll be right there with you, paddling, navigating the rough water, and guiding you through the process of mastering the river. I won't be your boss out there; I'll be your partner."

Hmm. I'd have to think on that a bit more. "Lastly," Tom ventured, "we must work together if we are to survive and thrive on our forays downriver. There will be loads of opportunity to laugh and have fun. Why would we do this if we couldn't enjoy it? We must support each other, and we work cohesively as a team in order for our trips to be successful. Tomorrow will be a full day, so I want you to fuel up. We're going to be expending a great deal of energy tomorrow, so you've got to be ready for that. Fuel isn't just about food. It's about resting and recharging. You'll do that too, starting tonight. Are there any questions?"

My friend raised her hand. "Tom, you forgot the last point on your list. What do you mean by, 'we have to trust the guide'?"

Tom laughed, almost as if he and my friend had rehearsed this beforehand. "Here's the thing. I suspect that none of you will even want to get into a raft with me if you don't trust me. Am I correct?" We all nodded in agreement. "Trust has to be earned, but it is also a mutually reciprocal contract. I realize that in order for the rafting trip to be successful, fun, and memorable, trust is the first thing that must be established. You need to trust me to keep you safe out there. If you can do that, you won't be overcome by anxiety when the water gets rough. When I bark out commands, you'll respond immediately instead of thinking, *I know better than this guy – I'll just do what I want.* Thinking like that might get us all killed. So, as your leader it is my responsibility to help you all to feel secure in my ability to keep you safe. Once we are in the boat, I am trusting all of you to trust me. That is the only way I'll be able to do my job with excellence – knowing that you feel safe enough with me to follow my lead as we navigate the rapids. So, team. Are you with me?"

A resounding cheer went up around the room. I headed off to bed that night thinking about Tom's rules for success in rafting, and wondered how I might apply them to the white waters I and my team were currently floundering in.

❧

AFTER AN EXHILARATING RIDE DOWN A SET OF RAPIDS, WE returned to the resort for some down time. I asked Tom if he would give me a few minutes of his time.

"I'm wondering, Tom, how do you manage to get a diverse group of people with varying backgrounds, levels of strength and ability to work so seamlessly together on the raft? I'm struggling with my team back home, and the stress of it is burning me out. You make it look so easy! What's your secret?"

He smiled and gestured for me to have a seat in a deck chair overlooking the river. "My secret is simple. Loving leadership."

Confused, I cocked my head to the side. "What do you mean? You love leadership? That's your trick?"

"No, my friend." He replied patiently. "Loving Leadership is what I call the way I work with people. I discovered long ago that the key to successful guiding is building a trusting relationship with my customers. I needed to find a way to establish rapport quickly, and to build a sense of safety and community so that they would work together on the river, much as you and your fellow rafters did today. I apply this same principle to the way I treat my staff. After all, the success of this business isn't just a matter of what I do; it depends on what we *all* do. My guiding team is out there on the water every day with rafters, just like I am. My sales and marketing teams have a tremendous impact on our ability to stay in business. We all have a part to play in making this venture successful."

He looked at me with sympathy in his eyes. "I used to be like you," he said. "I thought that everything in the business rode on my shoulders. That I was responsible for all the moving parts. I tried to micromanage everything, and the more I attempted to control my teams, the more we floundered and the more stress I felt. It wasn't until I realized that life on land is a lot like life on white water. Sometimes, the river is smooth, and you can just float along, but when the water gets rough, everyone needs to know what to do, how to do it, and they have to be willing to do it together. Otherwise, people get hurt, and the ride is a nightmare rather than a thrill ride."

I was intrigued. Leaning forward, I asked him, "Can you show me how your Loving Leadership concept works?"

"Absolutely." He smiled and produced his phone to show me a chart.

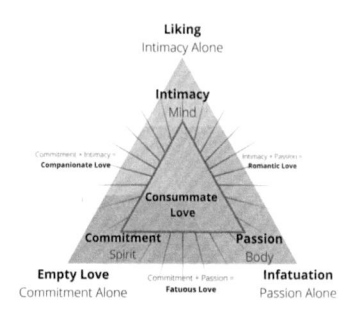

"This is Sternberg's triarchic theory of love[1]." He explained. "He suggested that love is made up of three key components: Intimacy, Passion, and Commitment. Intimacy is about the *mind*. Do you have things in common? Do you like each other? Do you trust each other? Do you feel safe with each other? Passion is about the *physical* connection, the spark, the attraction you feel towards another person. Finally, Commitment is about the *spirit*. It is that thing that makes you decide you want to remain engaged in the relationship, even to the point of forsaking all other relationships. Intimacy alone is just 'liking'; passion alone is 'infatuation', and commitment alone is 'empty'. But when you have all three components working together, you find 'the sweet spot' that is 'Consummate Love'."

Then Tom showed me another chart, explaining that this was Sternberg's theory adapted for the workplace.

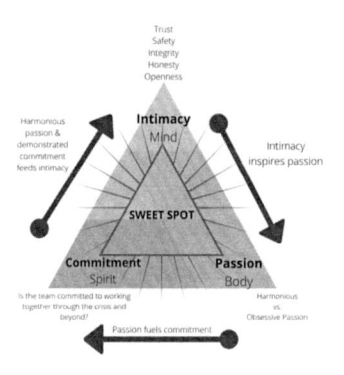

"In my conceptualization of Loving Leadership," Tom began, "I believe that a prosperous, productive, high-performing workforce also needs these three components of Intimacy, Passion, and Commitment. As an employer and as a guide, I need to develop rapport so that my teams feel like I am likeable. They need to trust me and feel safe with me. If they don't, it will be difficult to inspire passion in them, much like it would be hard for people to be physically passionate with each other if they don't like, trust or feel safe with their partner.

"Likewise, I need to trust them too, otherwise I will be afraid to work with them. They will sense my reticence and that too, will erode passion. The passion I want to spark in my business is harmonious passion. I want my staff and my clients to buy into the excitement of the work we do. They need to be passionate about working together and following the rules that keeps us all safe, because that's the only way we can have fun. Obsessive passion is overwhelming, consuming, and debilitating. It's what you're experiencing right now – the need to control everything – that's why you're here. Harmonious passion will enable you and your team to love your jobs and inspire the kind of engagement that is required to work through this crisis and any other challenge that comes after this one. When we have all three, we hit the sweet spot."

Tom continued, "When trust erodes, and people no longer feel safe, passion will fade and eventually die. Without intimacy and passion, you will be left with those people who remain committed only for the paycheque. That will leave you and the business coffers empty. So, my friend, if you want to rekindle the flames of passion so your team will remain engaged, begin at the beginning. Build intimacy."

"But how do I do that?" I asked in despair. We are expected to meet all these quotas and government expectations. How can I get them to trust me, when I am in a position to manage their work?"

Tom smiled wide. "You have found a part of your answer in the question you just asked. You've got to stop trying to *manage* people. It's time for you to *lead* them." Shifting in his seat, he gestured wide. "Since your people have transitioned to working from home, have productivity levels changed at all?"

I thought about it for a moment. "No, not really. The

numbers were not what they were supposed to be even before the pandemic."

"So," he surmised, "your attempts to micromanage their daily or weekly responsibilities have not boosted productivity at all."

"No... I suppose you're right in that." I replied.

"Let me ask you this. Do you trust your team? Do you believe them to be capable, qualified, intelligent people who understand the day-to-day requirements of their job? Do you trust them to do the work they have been tasked to do?" He smiled again. "Before you respond, really think about it. Some of your team likely have young children who are home schooling, or elderly parents who need caring for at home. Some may have parents in long-term care housing who are at higher risk for contracting this disease. They may be working in cramped quarters, sitting on furniture that is not ergonomically functional, with multiple distractions; yet their productivity has not fluctuated. What does that tell you?"

I felt like I had been sucker punched in the gut. It never occurred to me how shifting to virtual work might have impacted my team. All I was concerned about was the numbers. I forgot about my most valuable resource: my human resources. When I put everything Tom had said in perspective, I realized that I had no choice but to bestow more trust on my team. In spite of everything that could negatively impact their performance, they were still performing. So, if I looked at the common denominator in their progress, I had to admit that I was the weak link in the chain of high-performance.

"I understand now, Tom." I said to my guide. "I can't engender trust in my team if I don't start by trusting them to do their jobs. Micro-managing them and trying to direct all of their tasks makes them feel like I don't trust them. Why then would they feel safe with me? My actions are eroding trust, causing passion to fade, and lowering the commitment levels. What can I do to become a Loving Leader?"

"Come with me." Tom led me back into his office, where he handed me a sheet of paper with a list of strategies for becoming a Loving Leader.

1. Remember the rules for successful white water rafting. Prepare. Fuel up. Build trust. Share information. Stay on board and work together. Keep your eyes on the desired destination. Listen. Have fun! **When crises come, before you take action, perform a solution-focused cognitive appraisal with your team.** Include them in the process. Ask these questions:

- What is happening?
- What does it mean (for us, for the business, for the way we work)?
- How do I feel about it?
- What is our desired outcome? (Keep your eyes downriver)
- What options do we have to achieve that outcome?
- What is the best/worst thing that can happen if we choose option A, B, C, or D?
- What is the lifetime value of this event?

2. Hone your listening skills! Remember the team needs to know and understand the instructions so that when they hear them, they can listen and respond immediately. As a guide and a leader, you must also engage your listening skills – listen with the intent to understand rather than the intent to reply. Showing your team you care enough to really listen and hear what they are saying will build trust and strengthen intimacy.

3. Be transparent! Share information clearly and ensure

they all understand. If you don't know the answers, say so and promise to find out. If you're nervous about the unknown, be honest about it. Be an active participant in the process of change (like your rafting guide). Share your hopes for the future, and don't gloss over the challenges that you face. You're in this together. Show them that you rely on them just as they rely on you. Transparency feeds intimacy, fuels passion, and engages commitment.

4. Encourage! Catch your team members doing things right. Remember that navigating white water can be dangerous but it can also be fun! See the humour in things. Congratulate them for doing things well. Take an interest in their challenges and support them where you can. Work together to find solutions to problems that interfere with productivity. Ask for input and show gratitude when the team solves issues. Again, being an encouraging leader builds rather than erodes trust.

❧

"So," Tom concluded, "you can overcome the ill effects of future shock by developing a solid survival plan, and clearly communicating that plan. Demonstrate understanding & caring for your team. Working as a part of your team instead of standing apart from your team and applying the principles of Loving Leadership will help you build a sense of trust and safety. This will stoke the flames of passion, which increases engagement and commitment. The best part is that you will experience less stress and anxiety, and because you'll be experiencing harmonious passion as well as your team, you won't have to worry about burnout!"

I returned from that retreat feeling refreshed and empowered to be a different kind of leader – a Loving Leader. After three months of applying the principles Tom taught me, I found my team was happier, more present in their jobs, and our metrics for productivity were on the rise. Soon, we would be outperforming ourselves when we compared with metrics from the year before. Now that I see how Loving Leadership works, I'll never go back to "management" again.

7

CONNECTION TO YOUR PURPOSE AND YOUR WHY

Crystal-Lee Olson

I remember when I started my sales career, I was energetic, creative, and full of potential. I started from the ground up, at an entry-level sales position and thankfully, I worked within a large organization that allowed me to progress in my career every three years. I remember when I first started at that entry-level sales position, I had a dream and goal to work within the Corporate Accounts Department. At my first team Christmas party, I shared my dream of working within the Corporate Accounts Department, and the two leaders at the table asked me, "why did I want that?" I shared how much I loved helping our customers and wanted to make an even bigger impact. The two leaders were very quick to inform me that I had my head in the clouds, and that leadership at that level would not be something I would like. I did not care what they had to say; I knew that I would find a way to make it happen.

Within three years of working my way through two promotions, I found myself being presented with the oppor-

LEADERSHIP AIM

tunity to join the Corporate Accounts Department. The department had undergone a leadership transformation, and I saw this as my chance to shine and make the impact that I had desired. After two years of working within the department, I started to notice a shift and found the work to be less exciting, less challenging in the ways that I had imagined, and it had become more of what felt like a daily grind. I felt stuck and trapped especially when I entertained the idea of leaving the organization; I would find myself overwhelmed and paralyzed with fear.

I began to search for answers on how to fix this feeling of dissatisfaction with my work and position within the organization. I turned to my leaders within the organization, asking them for guidance on how to overcome this struggle. The leaders provided little insight and support on steps I could take to move forward. They too, were struggling with the overwhelm and a freight train that was roaring through the organization with a focus on the numbers and results. "Just stay focused on making sales," they encouraged.

In my own attempt to connect the dots, I looked at the company's core values and mission statement to find its purpose and the reasons why we got up and did our work in the world each day. It was here, in personal reflection and self-awareness, that I realized that my core values did not align with the way we did business. There was a misalignment.

I DID MORE OBSERVING WITHIN MY DEPARTMENT AND started to see what I perceived as a dysfunctional culture. I noticed that my team was focused on, 'what's in it for me', self-preservation, and working in silos. This started to make sense; of course, sales teams functioned this way. Each rep is given their territory - their land to master, govern, and reap the rewards from. Everything within my ten years of experience in sales was driven by results internally and externally. We only celebrated those who won or achieved bigger and better; there was no focus on growth, development, or truly functioning as a team. This felt wrong to me at my very core. I loved my colleagues and perceived them as not only as my team but an extension of my family. I knew I needed help unpacking this, so I reached out for external support to gain a better understanding of what I was experiencing and seeing.

I met with my coach, Shawnda for the first time with hope and aspirations of figuring out how to fix the dysfunctional culture, find the energy, creativity, and joy that I once had at work. Shawnda started by asking me about what I could do, or wanted to do, to make the necessary changes to re-ignite my passion. I remember thinking, what does passion have to do with my productivity, creativity, and enjoyment at work? I did not find the answers I wanted within that first session, but after a few weeks of working with Shawnda, I started to uncover and learn that you can tap into a powerful energy source when you connect with your purpose and why.

You are likely wondering what made me seek out support from a coach. How did I know that was the next best step I could take? This challenging and dissatisfying feeling was something new that I had not experienced before, and typically I never would have asked for help. My mentality in life and work was to figure it out on my own and just get it done. I stayed trapped in this feeling of discomfort and dissatisfaction with work for about a year before I reached out for help and support. I noticed I was getting caught in my thoughts and stewing in the discomfort. Sometimes I would reach out to friends or find a book to read, but none of that felt like it was helping.

I began to reflect on my successes, and noted that for

each of them, I recalled having a mentor or teacher to help me learn the knowledge and skills that were required to move forward. I had someone teach me in sports and school, then it dawned on me that I did not need to take this burden on my own, there was help and resources available, I just had to find them. It was always an option for me to spend more time learning and getting through this challenge on my own.

My pain and desire for improvement pulled me into wanting to create an experiment to see if there was a faster and easier way to get through to the other side of reclaiming my energy, creativity, and joy. I found this quote that truly inspired me during this time from Simon Sinek,[1] and it goes like this. "As the Zen Buddhist saying goes, 'How you do anything is how you do everything'". I knew I needed support and was willing to experiment with how to overcome this challenge, I did not want to leave my job or the organization.

During my next coaching session with Shawnda, she took me through an exercise called *Seven Layers Deep*[2]. The exercise was a process of her asking me seven questions, requiring me to dig deeper each time. She started with the first question, "Britney why do you want to continue to work in the Corporate Accounts team?" I responded with, "because I earn a good income, I enjoy the perks of the job, and I am financially comfortable." She continued asking me the next question "Why do you want to continue to earn a good living, enjoy the perks, and remain financially comfortable?" I responded, "because I worked hard to get to this point in my career and I am good at what I do."

Shawnda continued to ask questions each framed by my previous response. Finally arriving at the answer to question number seven to which I responded, "I do not want to experience undue suffering in my life. I want to be a leader." As those words left my mouth, I experienced a flood of emotions as I considered the time I had spent in this suffering state, all the lost creativity, and most importantly, the surge of energy I felt at the thought of becoming a leader. I had never thought that this was something I would want to do. All this time I was yearning for a sense of security, energy, and inspiration, and wishing I could trust my leaders and the team again. If I felt this way, I began to wonder how many other people in organizations were suffering in silence as I had been for so long?

☙❧

IT WAS THIS EXERCISE WHERE MY CONNECTION TO MY purpose and why became clear to me. I wanted to be a leader within the organization so that I could build a team and work environment that I believed would nurture a creative, successful, and energetic team. One that would not only produce the results that the organization required but exceed them. This is where I truly began to understand how the connection to our purpose and why provides strength and courage to continue to move forward despite difficult or challenging times. I felt energized by my purpose in becoming a leader, and my why was to dimmish or eliminate the possibility of undue suffering within the workplace. My purpose transformed into my vision of the future, and my why was the guide that led me towards that vision.

Shawnda shared a quote with me from Napoleon Hill's, *Think and Grow Rich*[3]. "There is one quality which one must possess to win, and that is the definitiveness of purpose, the knowledge of what one wants, and a burning desire to possess it". I had a burning desire to create a workplace that was inspiring, engaging, high performing, and secure because that was what I yearned for.

For the next four months, I continued to work with my coach, Shawnda, implementing the strategies, tools, and teachings into my work each day. I was strengthening relationships throughout the organization and seeing my energy, creativity, and joy slowly start to shift over these four months. Then, when one day my manager shared with me that he was planning to retire, I saw this as an opportunity to make my move. I asked if he would mentor me for an opportunity to fill his position. We worked together for six months, and I continued working with my coach, which lead me to successfully ending up as the new leader of the Corporate Accounts Department. I knew that my first task was to gather the team and begin to share what I had learned over the past ten months. We worked as a team on uncovering our department's purpose, why, and shared vision for our team and how our purpose and why would support the organization as a whole.

I believe that I would not have aspired to be an effective leader without the support and accountability from my coach Shawnda. My manager mentored me, and I had the option to model his leadership style and create the same results and culture that he did, or to create the change I desired to see. The coaching sessions made me more accountable in implementing the tools, strategies, and actions required to transform; it also gave me the time and space to show up for myself and discover the kind of leader I wanted to be. I relate my experience in working with coach Shawnda and the discovery to my purpose and why to push-ups. Everyone knows that they are a great exercise, and you will see results when you do them consistently, but when you are left to do push-ups on your own you may not implement the practice like you would when working with a trainer.

Shawnda's Insights

The connection to your purpose and your why is not just a power source to move you towards the future vision of your team or organization, it is the foundation or what one might describe as your North Star or compass to weather any storm i.e., changes and challenges. This North Star supports your character, builds trust, and enables you to build strong relationships. Brenee Brown defined the connection to your why as a requirement for creativity and innovation by going through the iteration of failure[4] (Brown, 2020). The connection between our purpose and our why is the life source of our ability to be able to get back up and try again despite repeated failure. Effective leaders use the lesson(s) or gift(s) from failure to ask powerful questions like "what's next vs what's wrong?"

Leadership is equivalent to an art form; like art, leadership is to produce work that inspires others and inspires change. The foundation of becoming an effective leader as shared in my story begins with self-awareness and working with a coach, which supports leaders to develop character, define the purpose, and the why. Some may perceive leadership as the mastery of skills that inspire others through character, trust, relationships, decision making, and communication; no matter what you identify as the key ingredients to effective leadership, the foundation still leads us all back to self-awareness. In knowing what inspires us as a leader will inspire and influence others through a shared vision. The connections to the purpose and the why will become our guiding North Star or compass in the creation of a shared vision. There is a great deal of supporting evidence within the research of leadership that closely connects to the clarity of vision and clarity of communication that nurtures the trust that is required in building effective teams and being an effective leader.

In 2009 TEDx released the Simon Sinek talk on *How*

LEADERSHIP AIM

Great Leaders Inspire Action[5]; it is in this talk that Sinek shares the pattern he recognized and defined as what great leaders and organizations do to create success and a loyal following. The pattern Sinek identified is a theory that he calls, "The Golden Circle" (see Figure 1). What he uncovered in his research was a pattern of communication used by leaders and organizations. The Golden Circle represents two ways of communication:

1. Outside in: What, How, and Why?
2. Inside out: Why, How, and What?

The order in which the communication flows makes the difference between great leaders and organizations – inside out vs. the most common way people communicate – outside in. What Sinek found was that inspired leaders communicated from the Why first, or in the terms of the Golden Circle, communication came from the inside out. Communication starts with the *why*, includes and expresses the purpose and beliefs; *how* explores the process or value proposition, and then *what* the organization does.

All people internally and externally can identify what an organization does, gain understanding and knowledge of how they do it; but without the why, leaders are unable to engage or gain loyalty from employees and customers. Sinek connects the proof to support the Golden Circle Theory with the biology of the human brain. The outer circle, "what" represents the neocortex; this is the source of rationalization, analytical thinking, and language. The two inner circles "how" and "why" represent the limbic brain, this is the part of the brain responsible for feelings, behaviours, decision making, but it does not understand language. How does this support organizational goals and success? Regardless of whether leaders are looking to gain loyal employees or customers, people are driven by shared beliefs – THE WHY.

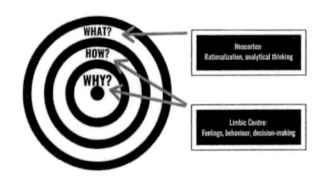

In Britney's story, the pivotal moment for her is uncovering her why, she shared in her story that she experienced a "flood of emotions" when discovering her why and connection to her purpose. Britney's leaders stopped communicating their purpose and why they do their work in the world; the leaders communicated and encouraged her to stay focused on the sales i.e., results. Without an understanding of the WHY, people within the organization cannot grasp the reasons for or a belief in why they should get out of bed to go to work. Our brains are pattern-seeking machines, constantly trying to make sense of our situations, conditions, and circumstances. This is what caused Britney so much suffering and loss of energy, creativity, and joy in her work.

Connection to the purpose and why is required especially now with so many leaders, teams, and individuals working remotely. The disconnection of human contact is putting leaders, teams, and individuals in new environments where a strong connection to the purpose and why is more important than ever. As a leader in this new world of virtual communicating and living, it is our responsibility to take the time to get clarity on the purpose and the why; start to share what we believe to inspire organizations and create the results that make positive impact in the world of work.

CALL TO ACTION:

1. Stay curious – What steps can you take to get clarity on your why and purpose?
2. Do your employees/team share the same beliefs?
3. How do you as a leader share and communicate the why, purpose, and vision?
4. Work with someone like a mentor or coach through the Seven Layers Deep exercise you can find online at www.thebetterlife.com – 7 Levels exercise sheet on the Book Resources tab (Graziosi, 2019).

8

COURAGEOUS LEADERSHIP

by Nance MacLeod

Persistence is the act of courage that gives you hope even when hope may not seem obvious.

Picture this: Toronto Ontario, 1988, growing financial institution. A 28-year-old woman named Christine Jung is moving up through the ranks in the corporate world; she finds herself in a senior executive role in less than five years after joining the company.

As she sits at her desk in her new executive office, she wonders, "Do I really belong here? Am I smart enough to do this work? Wow, this happened so fast! I am so proud that the company has so much faith in me, I hope I do not let them down."

This woman was me more than three decades ago.

※

AS I THINK BACK TO 1983, I WAS FRESH OUT OF UNIVERSITY and hoping to get an opportunity to work at a growing financial institution exactly like this one. I applied for an entry level Accounting Clerk position and after two interviews, I was offered the position. It was so exciting to have this opportunity. I was thrilled to the bone and maybe a little too proud of myself.

Within a few months of my new job, I noticed discrepancies in the accounting system. I spoke to my Dad who was my true hero in life, and he advised me to be 110% sure I knew all the facts and who was responsible. I should keep records, photocopies, all written communication, and keep clear notes. He referred to it as a CYA (cover your a$$) file.

He also told me to investigate on my own and to not bring anyone else into the investigation until I was sure whom I could trust completely. In fact he said, "Do not let anyone know what you are investigating, even people who you think are your friends".

I was surprised at what my Dad told me as I thought that I should go directly to my manager. This would be a perfect time to show him what a great accountant I am. My dad was insistent. He said, "In the corporate world when it comes to money, you cannot completely trust anyone. You must keep the honest people honest. Once you are sure and you have proof of what you suspect, go directly to the CEO. No one else. You do not want to be known as a snitch; no one needs to know."

As always, I heeded my Dad's words; after all, he is the smartest man I know, and he was the person who had directed me into my accounting career.

A few months later I had all the facts and evidence I needed, and it turned out to be my manager who was embezzling from the company; he had been for a long time. As always, my Dad had given me the right advice. I put together a portfolio with all the information and evidence I had discovered. I had my Dad review it, and with a few changes I was ready to present it to the CEO whom I had never met.

The CEO was Frederick Sanford, a man in his late 40's. He was well respected in the financial industry and was known for his business acumen as well as his big, welcoming smile. When he wanted something to happen, he made it happen. He often said, "Vision without execution is hallucination" (I believe this quote originated from Thomas Edison).

My mind raced and my heart felt like it was pounding loudly in my chest. At that time, I had only worked at the company for six months. How would I present this to Mr. Sanford? My manager had been with the company for almost fifteen years, he was well-liked and respected. Would Mr. Sanford believe me? Would he even look at the portfolio I worked so hard at putting together? Would he decide to fire me?" At this point I was feeling faint and I could hardly breathe.

I remembered what Dad said as I left his house. "When you have the best interests of the company in mind, you just need to take a deep breath and step through your fear, remember what fear is; False Evidence Appearing Real. He then quoted what Winston Churchill famously said, **'success is not final; failure is not fatal: it is the courage to continue that counts.'** "You have all the proof that your boss has been embezzling from the company. Your CEO is a smart businessman; he will appreciate your tenacity, persistence, determination, and honesty. My daughter, you are the most courageous girl I know."

As I remember all of this, I wonder why I was so nervous to speak to Fred way back then. Once I was in his office (which took a lot of negotiating with his secretary), I found him amazingly easy to talk to. He was incredibly open to what I told him, and when I handed him the portfolio with all the evidence, he seemed impressed as he flipped through it. He stood up and thanked me for bringing this to his attention and told me to leave it with him. He asked if I shared any of this with anyone else and I said just my Dad. He smiled his big friendly smile and told me again that he appreciated me being brave enough to come forward.

⚜

A DAY LATER, MY MANAGER WAS CALLED TO THE PERSONNEL office and he never returned to his desk. There were a lot of whispers and rumours. I listened to the things being said, but I did not say a word.

The next day I was called to the personnel office, my mind raced thinking that I had made a terrible mistake, I should have minded my own business. Stupid - stupid - stupid I said to myself. I took a deep breath and walked in the personnel office. Mr. Sanford was there with a big smile on his face and jumped up enthusiastically and shook my hand. I remembered that I was shaking, and that my hands were sweaty. I was somewhat embarrassed and blushed a little bit.

I was asked to sit down, Mr. Sanford said he reviewed my resume and spoke to my references, then asked me if ever led a team. I said that I led a team of volunteers at my church camp for several summers and I chaired several groups at University. That seemed to be enough for Mr. Sanford. After being in the company only six months, I was promoted to Manager of the Accounting department.

Speculation was flying around the organization as this was the first of many promotions for me. Fred insisted that I stopped calling him Mr. Sanford. He was not just the driving force for moving me forward successfully, but also a true mentor and friend. He taught me so much about business, strategy, vision, and financial management of the organization. We had regular weekly business meetings, and Fred was always interested in hearing my thoughts, ideas, and opinions.

I ignored the rumours that were spreading around the company. I worked hard and always treated my direct reports and peers with respect. My direct reports respected me and tried to shut down the talk. Most of my peers also knew that the rumours were not true. Fred was my mentor, and he took me under his wing as he saw potential in me, even though I was a young woman in a very male-dominated world.

I continued taking courses in leadership, human resources, organizational development, and corporate culture. I shared my vision and values to my direct reports and always asked for their input. Probably due to my inexperience and my persistence to be the best boss I could be, I turned around the accounting team's poor attitude. We worked closely together creating a vision for the department for all of them to work towards.

❦

BESIDES MY FORMAL EDUCATION, I LEARNED MUCH FROM Fred.

He taught me to never walk into his office with a problem if I did not have a few solutions to brainstorm with him.

He taught me to stand in my power and not allow anyone to treat me poorly; he told me what other people think about me is none of my business and that it has more to do with them than me.

He taught me to be authentic to who I am and to treat everyone with respect regardless of who they were and the position they held. Fred treated the janitor the same as he treated senior business leaders, with total respect.

He taught me the importance of turning strategy into reality; he always said execution is king, and that is what he respected most about me: even if something was really scary, I would always move forward and get it done. He knew that yes, I would be afraid at times and that I would push through my fear.

I shared my interest in engaging employees, creating positive corporate cultures, and the value of continuous learning and development. I talked about the importance of our employees; they are our most important asset. We were supposed to be in a "lean and mean era of business"; however, I knew this approach would not create success for our company. I pushed hard on this many times, and Fred was listening.

Next thing I knew, Fred created the brand-new position just for me *Chief Human Resource Officer.* He wanted me to have a seat at the executive table. This position that never existed before would replace the role of the Personnel Manager, who was retiring.

I found myself at this senior executive board table with six men in their late forties to early sixties, looking at me like I did not belong. After all, the Personnel Manager was never asked to sit at the board table. Why would they need a personnel manager at the table when the company is acquiring another financial institution?

I wondered if this was my own insecurities, until one of the male executives asked me, "Where is your note pad to take notes?"

Even though I felt like an imposter, I smiled gracefully and replied, "That is what Fred's Executive Assistant, Susan is here to do."

I worked hard not to take it personally; after all Fred did say that it would take the executive team some time to get used to having a woman at the board table. However, it was confusing to me as I worked hard to prove myself and the value I bring. These same men had always treated me in a friendly manner before, but now that I was sitting beside them making important decisions for the company, they treated me completely different. "What is that all about? Why do I make them so uncomfortable?" I wondered to myself.

During the first meeting, I was overly anxious to prove that I had value to add. I discussed the importance of strategies of building a positive corporate culture, introducing employee benefits, the importance of training and development, recruiting, onboarding, engaging, and motivating the employees, organizational effectiveness and development, especially as we were acquiring a whole new team.

After I spoke one of the older executives told me to "calm down" and "cool off" and even said that none of what I just said was important. He even suggested, "Why don't you be a good little girl and get us some fresh coffee?"

He told the executive team that as a woman, I just liked spending the company's money, and that there was no value in engaging the employees. After all, the key business strategies that were recommended right now in business were, "Lean and Mean".

I felt my cheeks get hot, and I knew I was turning red as I tried to keep my composure. I wondered "What would be the best way for me to respond?"

Before I could respond, Fred interjected. "Christine is not here to get us coffee, nor is she here to take notes; she is here because I believe we need her here. Christine is experienced, educated, and extremally valuable to this executive team, and we can all learn from her. She brings new ideas and strategies that will help this company grow as we move through change. I agree with her that we must keep our employees engaged and happy, and we must support them. Without our employees, we do not have a business.

"You all know profits have been slipping and growth is

stagnant in this company; that is why we decided to acquire another financial institution to help our growth and prosperity. We need Christine at this table. "

After Fred spoke, they all quieted down and moved on to a different discussion.

I became noticeably silent and only listened for the rest of the meeting.

I went back to my office and sat there wondering what I could have done differently. How could I do better at the next meeting? Maybe I needed to act and dress more like a man and that would get them to respect me. Should I become more aggressive, or was I too aggressive trying so hard to prove to them my value? It seemed that when men had new ideas and they were enthusiastic about them, they were perceived as smart, strategic, and respected. However, as a woman I was being labelled as too aggressive, loud-mouthed, and pushy.

As I sat in my new office, Fred came walking in with his big smile and said, "Well that went better than expected!"

I looked at him a bit distraught and asked, "What do you mean? That was terrible! They did not want to hear anything from me; they said I just wanted to spend their money, and all I was good for was to get them coffee and take notes."

He replied, "Hey Chris, you did great. These guys are not used to having a woman at the same level as them with new ideas, and they are feeling threatened. They do not see employees as the backbone of the company the way we do. Honestly, I didn't either until you made me realize that I was overlooking my most important assets - my employees. You are the most clever and fearless person I have ever met. You take on challenges with persistence, courage, and tenacity.

That is why you are in this position today. When you first walked into my office, I knew you were nervous. What impressed me most is that you stood in your power knowing that you were doing the right thing and you remained professional and respectful. I have full confidence that the executive team will see what I see. We will need to be patient. I want you to be yourself, stand in your power, just like you did when you walked into my office five years ago. "

I remember all of this like it was yesterday. It is hard to believe that was more than thirty years ago. I learned so much from Fred, he had much more confidence in me than I had in myself. He was right. I was able to gain respect from most of the executives around the table. There were still a few that seemed to dislike me, and I learned to accept that, since their dislike had more to do with their insecurities than my abilities. I worked at that company for fifteen years, and even though I had my challenges, the lessons I learned there were the most valuable of my life.

Now, we are closing out 2020, a year many consider the craziest year for all people and businesses internationally. There is this global pandemic that does not seem to want to end has resulted in lockdowns where many small businesses have to close their doors. There have been devasting fires destroying millions of acres in many different countries. There have been massive protests, civil unrest, crazy weather, a bitter election in the US, and murder hornets just to name a few of the challenges 2020 brought us.

The many lessons I learned in my thirty-plus years in senior leadership have supported the success of my organizations, especially in 2020.

1. To be a courageous leader you **must be persistent no matter how terrifying it might be to take action.** Persistence is the act of courage that gives you hope even when hope may not seem obvious. Always move through the fear with grace and respect and do what is right and honest. Set your goals, stick to the steps to make your goals a reality, remember life will have hardships, disappointments, discomfort, and uncertainty, but never let fear paralyze and stop you from moving forward. In 2020 we all needed to pivot, become creative, update our goals, figure out the new normal right now, and consider what the new normal will be in the future. Resilience has been one of the most used words in 2020; however, resilience is all about recovering quickly where persistence is continuing to move forward. I believe both words are important.
2. **Do not take anything people say to you or about you personally.** What they are saying has more to do with their character and little or nothing to do with you. Look quickly to see if there is a gold nugget learning opportunity in their comment. Do not waste too much time on it. It is easier said than done; we all want to be liked, appreciated, and valued. **How do you not take things personally?** I think my first lesson in not taking things personally was allowing myself to stand in my power, knowing my value. This does not mean to be arrogant; this means to know you are inherently worthy. I often think about what Mae West said, **"What other people think about you is none of your business."** I believe it is always a good idea to look for any value in

every negative comment. Learn and understand your own emotional triggers. This all helps, but the truth is we're all emotionally connected—especially when it comes to our family and friends—so we can't just not care. We can only manage our sensitivity and avoid taking things so personally that they hurt us for days or get us in a negative frame of mind. As Maya Angelou puts it, **"Your opinion is not the sum of me."**

3. **Be self-aware. Know your strengths, your weaknesses, and your saboteurs**. Always check in with yourself as you are always changing and learning. What is self-awareness really, and how do you know you are self-aware? Having your own personal mission and vision statement and knowing your core values, your drivers, and learning from your mistakes is all part of self-awareness. I believe that includes an honest self-appraisal about emotional strengths and vulnerabilities; your values and attitudes; personality traits and unresolved conflicts. You are a total person, not just a set of skills performing a role. This is where journaling comes in, as the more you self-reflect and challenge yourself by asking tough questions, the more layers of the self-awareness onion you will peel, getting to that rough diamond at the heart of you. I ask myself these questions every night: What worked today? What did not work today? What will I do better tomorrow? What emotional triggers were pushed today, and how did I respond or react? Did anything block me today from living life to its fullest? By asking myself these questions and

writing down the answers in my journal, it helps me to become more and more self-aware every day.

4. **Be your authentic self, always.** This allows richer interaction for giving feedback, sharing opinions, and ultimately having people believe in your passion and mission. You do not need to continually prove how smart you are; they will see it on their own. How do you be your authentic self? The funny thing about being authentic is that it is something you need to practice. Practice letting go of thinking you need to be all things to all people. You must truly "know thyself"; accept that each of us has a diamond in the rough inside of us; our job is to shine that diamond every day, presenting the best possible version of ourselves to the world. Practice authenticity by doing what is best for you, putting yourself first, and really understanding what is good for you. This attitude is not selfish; rather, it is truly selfless. I will quote from Marianne Williamson book, *A Return to Love*. **"There is nothing enlightened about shrinking so that other people won't feel insecure around you. We are all meant to shine, as children do. It's not just in some of us; it's in everyone. And as we let our own light shine, we unconsciously give other people permission to do the same. As we are liberated from our own fear, our presence automatically liberates others."** Also, as Henry David Thoreau said, **"Be yourself – not your idea of what you think somebody else's idea of yourself should be"**. Hiding behind a persona built on what you think you 'should' be, or

what you think will impress others will never bring you the peace to be authentic.

5. **Be a good listener — an active listener — a genuine listener.** Always listen to understand not to respond, listen with curiosity and with a beginner's mind. **How do you listen to understand and stop your brain from thinking about a response?** I remember reading in *The Seven Habits of Highly Effective People* by Stephen Covey, the importance of listening to understand rather than to respond. I understand that good communication starts with listening, but how do you get into this habit of not thinking about how to respond? I learned in my many coaching courses to be 110% focused on the person speaking, maintain eye contact, watch their body language, listen for inflections in their tone of voice, do not judge. Lean in, nod, and make the odd comment like really? Go on, or uh-huh when appropriate. Do not interrupt. Have a curious beginner's mind, and never assume you know more about a situation than the person speaking. Listen fully and only speak after they are done, reflect to them what you heard first, then ask questions to make sure you understand completely. Make sure there are no distractions, shut off your cell phone and email message alerts or anything else that will take your attention away from the person speaking. Digital distractions are one of the major threats to communication in the 21st century. Practice your listening skills every day in every setting until they become natural to you.

6. **Never Stop Learning.** It is essential to seek out mentors, industry resources, and development

tools to grow your social capital in both personal and professional development. Never stop learning! Lifelong learning is important to your success, and we all must remember even though our brain is an organ, it acts more like a muscle: the more you use it, the stronger it becomes. You know the saying, "Use it or lose it"!

9

GETTING OUT OF YOUR OWN WAY – THE PRACTICE OF LEADERSHIP FLOW

By Tanya Smith

"Hey, Jackson...over here!"

I looked past the long lineup at the lunch buffet table to a table in the outdoor courtyard – a familiar face was waiting for me to join her at the table – Isabella. Isabella and I had been colleagues for many years in the same government department. We both worked our way up the chain of command, and then Isabella moved to a different region. Now we meet up once a year at this annual conference. In the past, I've enjoyed spending time catching up and sharing stories of bad bosses, underperforming employees, disgruntled unions, and what-have-you with Isabella. This year would be different considering my recent shift in leadership style. Silently, I thought to myself, "This is going to be interesting."

I approached the table and was welcomed by Isabella.

"Great to see you," Isabella said. "I was wondering whether you were here this year. I was hoping so as I always enjoy catching up with you and sharing stories.

"What did you think about that last session on leadership styles? What are your thoughts on the facilitator's invitation to think about 'How we get in our own way' when it comes to leadership?"

I took a seat. After the preliminary "hellos" and general catch up with the others on their families, the conversation turned to our usual style of conversation – what could be referred to as leadership war/horror stories. Isabella started sharing stories about how either her staff, her boss, or the administration continued to get in her way of achieving results and getting things done since they last saw each other. I knew this story all too well. It was the same story I had been telling others (and myself) for twenty plus years. It is my story, and I want to think that it is also history in my life as a Public Sector Executive leader.

I started in the public sector right out of university. I worked my way up the ladder working for demanding and commanding style bosses who taught me the importance of achieving results and meeting goals. This was the style of leadership I was familiar with and the one I modeled (unconsciously) as I took on roles with increased responsibility in the public sector. This was the leadership style I was attracted to. It provided me the recognition I understood to be important in the workplace – deliver and done. The wake you leave doesn't matter – it isn't measurable, and you are paid to produce.

This all changed when Amir arrived as my new boss.

"Jackson, what do you think? Are you getting in your own way? What does that even mean? Aren't we paid to get the job done?" Isabella was directing her rhetorical questions at me. Here was my opening I thought – am I going to be courageous enough to start "THIS" conversation with her. Was I going to show up today, at this moment, and share my experience over the last year? Was I going to get out of my own way and share with her the details of my current journey?

Amir was a veteran executive with 30+ years of experience in the "field" and "in HQ". He was known for being well-liked. My reputation was different. I was known for being bossy, opinionated, and "not a people person". I ran my shop with a heavy hand and recognized those who "showed up, kept up and shut up". I got things done. I was of the school of management thinking that work was done at the workplace and your personal baggage was to be left at the door – preferably outside the office door. There was no room at the office for personal lives. Work was a place for thinking and action – not a place where emotions were discussed.

Right from our first meeting, I knew it was going to be different with Amir. He asked me questions – he was curious about my values, and he wanted to know how I built a trust relationship with my team, my colleagues, my previous bosses. He shared his values with me – he valued authenticity, he valued compassion, he valued making a difference and he valued humour and having fun. What kind of meeting was that? He did not ask me about my results, my priorities. HE gave me a book to read! I left the meeting frustrated and confused.

A few weeks passed and I had other meetings where Amir was present. When he chaired the meeting, he started by asking participants to share what was important to them at this moment, what was important about this meeting for them and he invited (his words not mine) participants to be open and honest about any distractions they needed to take care of so they could be fully present to the meeting. He asked questions of participants – what wins and what challenges did they have, what support did they need, what were they doing to create fun and engagement in the work environment, and what commitments they were making to the team vis-à-vis tasks between now and the next meeting. He shared his own wins/challenges, the support he needed from us (his team), made commitments for his own deliverables. I felt like I was in another world. My curiosity started to kick in...how does he DO this?

"So, Jackson, tell me what has been happening in your world back at the office." I returned my attention to the conversation with my former colleague.

"Well Isabella, I have had quite a year. I discovered exactly what the last facilitator was referring to...that I was getting in my own way and I also realized that I needed to do something about it. Fair warning, the villain in my story this year, is not a disgruntled, underperforming employee or a "let's play nice HR administrator", or a boss that lacks vision and direction. The villain this year is me."

My curiosity was increasing every time I met with Amir.

He never once directed me to do something. He asked me lots of questions and not once did he provide a direct solution. Finally, about a month into our new relationship I decided I needed to know how he was "doing" this.

And this is what I learned...Amir's story started when he was introduced to his competency development coach. Amir was noticing that he was getting in his own way and wanted to figure out how he could do things differently. He figured that the coach would tell him exactly what he needed to do and then he would just implement.

Amir shared that what followed was not exactly what he was expecting. His coach invited him to take a pause- to slow down from "doing", and to spend time reflecting. Amir could tell by the look on my face that I was not quite sure what this invitation meant.

"My coach, he said, gave me three questions to start me off. The three questions were: 1) what is working with your current leadership style and why? 2) what isn't working about your current leadership style and why? And 3) what do you want to be different and why?"

Amir asked if I would be interested in "playing" with those questions and I accepted the challenge. He offered that when he did this exercise, he scheduled a pause at midday and the end of his day to intentionally reflect/think about the questions and record his thoughts. I committed to doing the same. My curiosity piqued; what would I discover?

"Wow - This year's story is quite different than your previous stories, Jackson" Isabella remarked. I nodded my agreement and continued to share what I had discovered about myself and my leadership style in the past year.

I disclosed to Isabella that I had discovered by slowing down in the moment to reflect, that I could make better choices about my leadership behaviours. I discovered that every situation may require a different response. I discovered that I and others all have different needs, and to be in service to others required me to be able to adapt and flex my leadership style in the moment.

I drifted back in my thoughts to what happened next for me.

The next few meetings with Amir were focused on my discoveries from my reflections and Amir offered up the next step to practice shifting from the "doing" mode to the "being" mode of leadership. The next step Amir referred to was **intention**. *He asked me which discovery from question 3 - What do you want to be different and why? - I would be interested in acting on, and he invited me to set an intention and to practice "being". I chose that I wanted to practice curiosity with my team – I felt that this was the quality that most intrigued me about Amir's leadership style, and I felt it might support me to shift from solutions mode to options mode with my team. With Amir's help, I came up with my intention and how I would practice. I planned to take a pause by taking three breaths and say to myself "I am curious" before I started a meeting and/or conversation with any member of my team.*

I practiced this pause/intention for a few weeks and noticed a difference however I felt that I needed something else to take it to the next level. Something was missing. I returned to Amir and he was excited when I told him about what I was experiencing. During the conversation, Amir shared the last element of the model that he referred to as his "Leadership Flow" model...first comes **Reflection**, *followed by **Intention**, and then there is **Action**. Again, he reminded me that action in this way is a bit different, and he encouraged me to practice exploring what action would look like for me regarding my work in strengthening my curiosity muscles with my team. He offered that perhaps action in this situation was for me to act with my language. He invited me to start to play with incorporating some different language into my conversations with my team. We brainstormed and came up with some examples, such as "I am curious to know..." "Tell me more about..." "What would you do now...?" "How would you approach this...?" and I committed to trying them out.*

He acknowledged my courage to try something new, and he cautioned me that this would take discipline on my part. He went on to share that his coach had offered him three rules to support him with practicing action which he shared with me: Start Slow – try one new thing at a time and think about how it supports you. Be Kind to Yourself – this is key as you may be learning something new. Start Again – he referenced this as the most important rule, noting that improvement/change will only come with practice, which grants you permission to start over.

"Come on Jackson...did that actually work?" Isabella asked with bewilderment.

"I know Isabella, it sounds crazy and falls into that "touchy-feely" stuff that I have mocked before. I was amazed how powerful it was, and I liked how I felt at the beginning, during, and at the end of these meetings/conversations. In a few weeks of practicing, I discovered that my team members wanted to be involved, and they had ideas, options, and solutions to problems. I found they were more engaged, and this supported an increase in productivity. Deadlines were being met or exceeded, and the quality of the work being produced improved. They were leaving meetings or conversations excited to do the work they needed to do. And do you remember last year, I was having challenges with Jacques, my manager – we were constantly in a combative stance with each other – I felt he was always getting in our way of progress, he was always pointing out risks and telling me why we couldn't do things. Well, that relationship has completely changed. I realized that my leadership style and behaviours were getting in the way of his success, and I now realize the value he brings to the team.

"And I feel different...I feel many things and to name just a few...I feel less stressed about the workload (I do not feel that it rests all on my shoulders). I feel less stressed about the performance of my team (productivity and work quality had both increased). My performance anxiety has decreased as I do not always have to provide the solution. I can rely on others to find solutions.

"I have had a great year and so has my team. Team retention rates have increased and in the last three months more people have been requesting to work with us!

"Isabella, I have to say...the bottom line is that I recognized that I was 'getting in my own way'. It was all about me. I needed to tune into who I am; I needed to understand how my behaviours impact others, and I had to learn how to adapt (in the moment) to make my environment more efficient, effective, and enjoyable.

"I learned I needed to be in 'Leadership Flow'. I continue to practice (or as Amir refers to it as "play") with the three elements: Reflection, Intention, and Action. I continue to use the elements to work on strengthening other leadership competencies/qualities in myself that I have decided I want to change. I have also learned that this is not easy work. There is no magic wand for this work. I don't have the same needs and wants as everyone else, and the work begins and ends with conscious awareness. Achieving leadership flow is intentional work and takes practice. And it comes with rewards... they just aren't measured the same way I measured my success in the past."

"Jackson – this is super interesting, and you've got me interested. I think I want to try it out. Can you send me a note outlining the three elements and some guidance on how to get started?" Isabella asked, reaching her hand out to me. Our annual lunch together finished with a smile and a handshake. I felt good about being honest with Isabella about my learnings in the last year.

I took her hand. "Isabella – it would be my pleasure, and I can't wait to hear about your discoveries next year."

THE PRACTICE OF LEADERSHIP FLOW: DEVELOPING Leadership Competencies in the 21st Century
Reflection Practice

Decide on a leadership competency/quality that you want to strengthen.

Split your day into three equal parts. At the end of each period, take the time to answer the questions below. Reflect on what you have experienced within yourself as well as on what you have revealed to the world around you. Write your observations in your journal so that you may discover the trends that emerge.

Part A:

1. What is working for you with regards to this leadership competency/quality and why?
2. What is not working for you with regards to this leadership competency/quality and why?
3. What do you want to be different about this leadership competency/quality and why?

Part B:
Once a week, review your notes considering the following:

1. What did I learn about myself?
2. What new possibilities unfold for me?

Duration: 2 weeks
Source: Adapted from Integral Development Coaching Program – New Ventures West

INTENTION PRACTICE

Based on any new possibilities that unfolded for you during the reflection exercise, decide on an intention you want to set for yourself. Intentions are modeled using "I am..." statements (example: you decide you want to strengthen your curiosity muscle/competency and therefore your intention would be stated as "I am curious.").

To practice your intention before an activity, follow the steps below:

1. Stop what you are doing.
2. Take three mindful breaths (inhale through the nose and exhale through the mouth). *
3. Silently state your intention to yourself.
4. Commence activity.
5. Journal about your experience after the activity.

Guiding questions for journaling activity:
What did I learn about myself?

1. What did I learn about others?
2. What new possibilities unfold for me?

*Note: Pausing to take three breaths is important to this practice and it is not recommended that you skip this step of the practice. This mindful breathing will allow you to ground yourself and become aware of your thoughts, feelings, and sensations in the moment. This breathing allows you to become present.

Duration: 2 weeks

Action Practice

Action is all about practicing something new. Decide / Choose a competency you want to strengthen or deepen. Brainstorm activities/actions you could implement to be able to practice strengthening your selected competency. Set a goal for yourself and begin to practice.

Rules for Practicing

1. Start Slow
2. Try one new thing/activity at a time.
3. Reflect on how it supported you.
4. Adjust, as required.
5. Be Kind to Yourself
6. You may be learning something new and recognize that it takes time and energy.
7. Treat yourself like you would treat a friend who is trying something new.
8. Start Again
9. We all get knocked off balance and when that happens with what you are trying permit yourself to start/try again.

Duration: 2 weeks

"A conscious leader is someone who leads with conscious awareness. Conscious awareness is a process of recognizing what is going on inside and out, the effects of decisions and actions, and the interaction between a complex array of factors and forces."

Jeff Klein, Chief Executive Officer of Working for Good

RE-CAPPING THE WISDOM FROM LEADERSHIP AIM

by Nance MacLeod

Now, it is time to review all the wonderful wisdom shared by our contributors.

We start with Sandra Cabal's Leadership Road Trip – in which she introduced Executive Coach Global's proprietary leadership and team engagement model, The Seven Fundamentals of Leadership and Team Engagement. You have seen elements of these seven fundamentals woven throughout this book.

The Seven Fundamentals of Leadership and Team Engagement:

1. **Gaining trust.** Members of great teams trust one another on a fundamental emotional level. They are comfortable sharing their weaknesses, mistakes, fears, behaviours, and challenges. They get to a point where they can be completely honest without filters.
2. **Communicating for transparency.** Leaders

who communicate well, build on trust and respect. Two-way communication is vital to ensure members feel listened to and valued. This is a core value that drives innovation and team development for retention and performance.

3. **Earning respect.** Mutual respect generates passionate dialogue about issues and decisions that are key to the organization's success. This drives conversation around better solutions, best answers, discovering truths and making great decisions.
4. **Building resilience.** Resilience does not come easily but there are ways to cultivate it. During times of uncertainly and crisis knowing you can build your resilience by being open to change, aware of increasing levels of anxiety, fully engaged, present and active, practicing self-compassion and gratitude.
5. **Managing change.** the pace of change has accelerated greatly. Leaders need to face and manage change in a constructive way and be adaptable, agile, and creative. Learning how to lead your team though change will ensure successful outcomes and productivity.
6. **Coaching with compassion.** A coaching culture drives engagement, productivity, and accountability. Leaders who are trained as compassionate coaches inspire meaningful conversations to build trust, strong relationships, create respect and hopefulness and bridge communication gaps. Successful leaders of winning teams have a trusted coach and mentor and the basic skills to lead as a coach.
7. **Achieving results.** Leaders who inspire their team, provide purpose and show what is possible

achieve amazing results and scale to new heights. Being creative, agile and coming up with great strategies is great but execution trumps everything.

Sandra further shares the wisdom of a Kaizen facilitator:

1. **Be Present Not Just Seen**. Managers had always been expected to be present on the shop floor. In reality, they met this obligation by being seen; walking as quickly as possible with head down to avoid eye contact and any potential interaction. Being present, means to be involved and establish relationships.
2. **Listen & Learn**. Going back to my life lesson about listening, this point was my contribution to our behavioral map to success. Leaders invested the time to listen and to learn. They brought knowledge to each other, sharing experiences, learning from the employees, their representatives, and each other.
3. **Act with Integrity**. Integrity is the act of behaving honorably even when no one is watching. Acting with integrity meant our decisions needed to follow moral and ethical principles that facilitated inclusion. In other words, taking the easy way out was not an option.
4. **Become a Coach, Develop a Team.** The leadership team seized coaching opportunities that supported the first steps towards developing a positive culture.
5. **Give and Receive Feedback**. Partnerships occur when two or more parties engage in the same

activity. It happens when everyone is moving in the same direction.

※

Surviving the Sharks in Suits

In Chapter Two, Alexander Lutchin takes you through several scenarios as his avatar Robert K.C. Smith. Some of you may have experienced Sharks in Suits of both genders in your career. Here are some keys to surviving the shark-infested waters of the business world.

1. Use situational awareness, actively listen, ask lots of questions, know and assert your value.
2. Personality trumps performance: create strong relationships horizontally and vertically, identify the influencers and create your circle of influence.
3. Identify several powerful mentors inside and outside your organization to mentor you and hire an executive coach to support your success.
4. Be involved socially. Get to know people on a personal level, engaging socially with your circle of influence.
5. Understand Emotional Intelligence and hone your own self-awareness and soft skills.
6. Learn basic coaching core skills like actively listening, being curious and asking thought provoking questions with compassion and no judgement.
7. Keep yourself in a Positive Emotional Attractor (PEA) mindset.
8. Learn how to help others from being in a Negative Emotional Attractor (NEA), and support them

moving into a Positive Emotional Attractor (PEA) mindset.
9. People will not remember what you said but they will always remember how you made them feel.

❦

Leading with Empathy

In our third chapter, Aline Ayoub introduces us to Xavier French and how he created a brand-new avatar when he realized he needed to rewire his leadership style and re-engineer his playbook as a leader.

The core aspects of Xavier's transformation lay in these processes:

1. **Self-Reflection** and understanding his own core values. Reflecting on how to be a better leader, a better father and how to connect and engage the team by showing them his empathy for them.
2. **Engaging** in transparent communication in all his relationships.
3. **Knowing** that as a leader he needed to adapt, innovate and have a people-centric approach.
4. **Understanding** the challenges, strengths and weaknesses existing in him and his team. Understanding that people listen with their emotions. The head does not hear until the heart has listened.
5. **Admitting** that he did not know-it-all, treating failures as learning opportunities.
6. **Welcoming** diverse perspectives and choosing to respond positively to change and challenges.
7. **Listening** without judgement, makes room for harnessing new ideas.

8. **Gaining trust** with open communication by being transparent, consistent, and human.
9. **Challenging** himself as a leader everyday.
10. **Being** an empathetic leader can heal a dysfunctional team.

Unlearning Learned Behaviour

In Chapter Four, we meet a young female finance executive whose misguided attempts to follow her father's outcome-driven footsteps led to her making some life-altering mistakes that affected her family and her leadership success. She learned to unlearn certain principles and came to acknowledge the importance of:

1. Finding a balance. The professional and personal, work and home, mental and physical, are not mutually exclusive.
2. Recognizing the impact that major changes would have on the people involved and their families, customers and the company's reputation as a local employer.
3. Treating employees with respect and trusting them in order to build a successful business.
4. Working with a cohesive team and maintaining a wholistic view of all processes.

As leaders and role models, we must be keenly aware that how we show up and how we behave directly affects business results.

The FIVE factors used for a successful acquisition or merger are:

1. People Impact
2. Employee Experience
3. Productivity, Safety
4. Employer Reputation
5. Customer Relations

※

The Emotionally Intelligent Leader

Wendy Woods's avatar comes to realize the value of developing Emotional Intelligence as a leader. Her avatar learns that lack of emotional self-awareness (ESA) is the foundation upon which the other fourteen EQ competencies are built; without it, it is impossible to boost your EQ.

The key strategies and actionable steps from the avatar's experience are as follows:

1. Develop situational awareness, how is my team responding to me?
2. Mindfulness exercises can be used to support ESA.
3. Ask an accountability partner to hold you accountable to completing your mindfulness practice and any other EQ development strategies.
4. Stop what you are doing for a minute.
5. Take a few deep breaths and notice as it comes in and out of your nose.
6. Observe your thoughts, feelings, and body sensations.
7. Proceed with something that will support you in the moment, like a cup of tea, or a grounding activity.

※

Loving Leadership

In this chapter Julie A. Christiansen takes you on a whitewater rafting adventure and introduces you to Sternberg's triarchic theory of love and the adapted proprietary model Loving Leadership Taxonomy. She shares strategies for overcoming the ill effects of "future shock".

Here is a snapshot of the wisdom in this chapter:

1. **Remember the rules for successful whitewater rafting.** Prepare. Fuel up. Build trust. Share information. Stay on board and work together. Keep your eyes on the desired destination. Listen. Have fun!
2. **When crises comes before you take action, perform a solution-focused cognitive appraisal with your team.** Include them in the process. Ask these questions: What is happening? What does it mean (for us, for the business, for the way we work)? How do I feel about it? What is our desired outcome? (Keep your eyes downriver). What options do we have to achieve that outcome? What is the best/worst thing that can happen if we choose option A, B, C, or D? What is the lifetime value of this event?
3. **Hone your listening skills!** Remember the team needs to know and understand the instructions so that when they hear them, they can listen and respond immediately. As a guide and a leader, you must also engage your listening skills – listen with the intent to understand rather than the intent to reply. Showing your team you care enough to really listen and hear what they are saying will build trust and strengthen intimacy.
4. **Be transparent!** Share information clearly and

ensure they all understand. If you don't know the answers, say so and promise to find out. If you're nervous about the unknown, be honest about it. Be an active participant in the process of change (like your rafting guide). Share your hopes for the future, and don't gloss over the challenges that you face. You're in this together. Show them that you rely on them just as they rely on you. Transparency feeds intimacy, fuels passion, and engages commitment.
5. **Encourage!** Catch your team members doing things right. Remember that navigating white water can be dangerous but it can also be fun! See the humour in things. Congratulate them for doing things well. Take an interest in their challenges and support them where you can. Work together to find solutions to problems that interfere with productivity. Ask for input and show gratitude when the team solves issues. Again, being an encouraging leader builds rather than erodes trust.

※

Connection to Your Purpose and Your Why

In Chapter Seven Crystal-Lee Olson shares the power of the connection to your purpose and your why, referring to Simon Sinek's "The Golden Circle Model". The connection to your purpose and your why is not just a power source to move you towards the future vision of your team or organization, it is the foundation or what one might describe as your North Star or compass to weather any storm i.e., changes and challenges. This North Star supports your character, builds trust, and enables you to build strong relationships.

How to connect to your purpose and your WHY:

1. Stay curious – What steps can you take to get clarity on your why and purpose?
2. Build trust with your team by sharing your purpose and why.
3. Do your employees/team share the same beliefs? Do they know their purpose and why?
4. How do you as a leader share and communicate the why, purpose, and vision? Share authentically with candor and kindness.
5. Work with someone like a mentor or coach through the Seven Layers Deep exercise you can find online at www.thebetterlife.com

Courageous Leadership

In Chapter Eight, I share the story of Christine Jung, who struggled with imposter syndrome, untrue nasty rumours as well as navigating a male dominated board table.

The key leadership lessons from this chapter:

1. To be a courageous leader you **must be persistent no matter how terrifying it might be to take action**. Persistence is the act of courage that gives you hope even when hope may not seem obvious. Always move through the fear with grace and respect and do what is right and honest. Set your goals and stick to the steps to make those goals a reality. Resilience has been one of the most used words in 2020; however, resilience is all about recovering quickly where persistence is continuing to move forward. I believe both attributes are important.

2. **Do not take anything people say to you or about you personally**. Look quickly to see if there is a gold nugget learning opportunity in their comment. Do not waste too much time on it. Remember what Mae West said, "What

other people think about you is none of your business." It is always a good idea to look for the inherent value in every negative comment. **Learn and understand your own emotional triggers.**

    3.**Be self-aware.** Know your strengths, your weaknesses, and your saboteurs. Always check in with yourself as you are always changing and learning. Having your own personal mission and vision statement and knowing your core values, your drivers, and learning from your mistakes is all part of self-awareness. Conduct an honest self-appraisal about emotional strengths and vulnerabilities; your values and attitudes; personality traits and unresolved conflicts. Use journaling as a tool for ongoing self-reflection. Ask yourself these questions every night: What worked today? What did not work today? What will I do better tomorrow? What emotional triggers were pushed today, and how did I respond or react? Did anything block me today from living life to its fullest? By asking yourself these questions and writing down the answers in a journal, you can become more self-aware every day.

    4.**Be your authentic self, always**. This allows richer interaction for giving feedback, sharing opinions, and ultimately having people believe in your passion and mission. Authenticity requires practice! Practice letting go of thinking you need to be all things to all people. Practice authenticity by doing what is best for you, putting yourself first, and really understanding what is good for you. This attitude is not selfish; rather, it is truly selfless. Marianne Williamson said, "There is nothing enlightened about shrinking so that other people won't feel insecure around you. We are all meant to shine, as children do. It's not just in some of us; it's in everyone. And as we let our own light shine, we unconsciously give other people permission to do the same. As we are liberated from our own fear, our presence automatically liberates others."

5.**Be a good listener — an active listener — a genuine listener.** Always listen to understand not to respond, listen with curiosity and with a beginner's mind. Stephen Covey expresses the importance of listening to understand rather than to respond. Good communication starts with listening. You can accomplish this by being 110% focused on the person speaking, maintaining eye contact, watching their body language, listening for inflections in their tone of voice, and not judging. Have a curious beginner's mind, and never assume you know more about a situation than the person speaking. Digital distractions are one of the major threats to communication in the 21st century. Practice your listening skills every day in every setting until they become natural to you.

6.**Never Stop Learning.** It is essential to seek out mentors, industry resources, and development tools to grow your social capital in both personal and professional development. Never stop learning! Lifelong learning is essential to your success; remember that even though your brain is an organ, it acts more like a muscle: the more you use it, the stronger it becomes.

❦

Getting Out of Your Own Way – The Practice of Leadership Flow

In Chapter Nine, Tanya Smith's avatar, Jackson learned a new Leadership style from his boss Amir, who taught him the process called, "Leadership Flow". The key elements are as follows:

LEADERSHIP AIM

1. **Self Reflection** creates Self Awareness; this is the foundation of being a good leader by gaining trust.
2. **Living with Intention** every minute of every day. Communicating for transparency, earning trust, building resilience, and managing change will all happen naturally when lining with intention.
3. **Captivating Action** this is the opposite of being bossy, this is coaching with Compassion and Achieving results

The following practices will support your own Leadership Flow.

Reflection Practice
Decide on a leadership competency/quality that you want to strengthen.

Split your day into three equal parts. At the end of each period, take the time to answer the questions below. Reflect on what you have experienced within yourself as well as on what you have revealed to the world around you. Write your observations in your journal so that you may discover the trends that emerge.

Part A:

1. What is working for you with regards to this leadership competency/quality and why?

2. What is not working for you with regards to this leadership competency/quality and why?

3. What do you want to be different about this leadership competency/quality and why?

Part B:

Once a week, review your notes considering the following:

1. What did I learn about myself?
2. What new possibilities unfold for me?

Duration: 2 weeks

Intention Practice

Based on any new possibilities that unfolded for you during the reflection exercise, decide on an intention you want to set for yourself. Intentions are modeled using "I am..." statements (example: you decide you want to strengthen your curiosity muscle/competency and therefore your intention would be stated as "I am curious.").

To practice your intention before an activity, follow the steps below:

1) Stop what you are doing.

2) Take three mindful breaths (inhale through the nose and exhale through the mouth). *

3) Silently state your intention to yourself.

4) Commence activity.

5) Journal about your experience after the activity.

Guiding questions for journaling activity:

What did I learn about myself?

What did I learn about others?

What new possibilities unfold for me?

Duration: 2 weeks

Action Practice

Action is all about practicing something new. Decide / Choose a competency you want to strengthen or deepen. Brainstorm activities/actions you could implement to be able to practice strengthening your selected competency. Set a goal for yourself and begin to practice.

Rules for Practicing

1) Start Slow

   a. Try one new thing/activity at a time.

   b. Reflect on how it supported you.

   c. Adjust, as required.

2) Be Kind to Yourself

    a. You may be learning something new and recognize that it takes time and energy.

    b. Treat yourself like you would treat a friend who is trying something new.

3) Start Again

    a. We all get knocked off balance and when that happens with what you are trying permit yourself to start/try again.

Duration: 2 weeks

QUOTES FROM LEADERSHIPAIM

"A conscious leader is someone who leads with conscious awareness. Conscious awareness is a process of recognizing what is going on inside and out, the effects of decisions and actions, and the interaction between a complex array of factors and forces."
   Jeff Klein, Chief Executive Officer of Working for Good

"Even though our brain is an organ, it acts more like a muscle: the more you use it, the stronger it becomes. You know the saying, "Use it or lose it"!
   Nance MacLeod, Chief Coaching Officer

"There is nothing enlightened about shrinking so that other people won't feel insecure around you. We are all meant to shine, as children do. It's not just in some of us; it's in everyone. And as we let our own light shine, we unconsciously give other people permission to do the same. As we are liberated from our own fear, our presence automatically liberates others."
   Marianne Williamson book, A Return to Love.

"Be yourself – not your idea of what you think somebody else's idea of yourself should be."
   Henry David Thoreau

"Listen to understand, not to respond."
   Stephen Covey

"You are a total person, not just a set of skills performing a role."
   Nance MacLeod, Chief Coaching Officer

"Your opinion is not the sum of me."
   Maya Angelou

"What other people think about you is none of your business."
   Mae West

"Resilience has been one of the most used words in 2020; however, resilience is all about recovering quickly where persistence is continuing to move forward. I believe both words are important."
   Nance MacLeod, Chief Coaching Officer

"Success is not final; failure is not fatal: it is the courage to continue that counts."
   Winston Churchill

"To be a courageous leader you must be persistent no matter how terrifying it might be to take action. Persistence is the act of courage that gives you hope even when hope may not seem obvious."
   Nance MacLeod, Chief Coaching Officer

"Vision without execution is hallucination."
   Thomas Edison

"In the corporate world when it comes to money, you cannot completely trust anyone. You must keep the honest people honest."
Gordon MacLeod

"The connection between our purpose and our why is the life source of our ability to be able to get back up and try again despite repeated failure. Effective leaders use the lesson(s) or gift(s) from failure to ask powerful questions like "what's next vs what's wrong?"
Crystal-Lee Olson

*There is one quality which one must possess to win, and that is the definitiveness of purpose, the knowledge of what one wants, and a burning desire to possess it."
Napoleon Hill*

"When we take the time to consider the people aspects upfront, then the success will follow."
Michele Bush

"How you do anything is how you do everything."
G. Martinengo

"When trust erodes, and people no longer feel safe, passion will fade and eventually die. Without intimacy and passion, you will be left with those people who remain committed only for the paycheque. That will leave you and the business coffers empty. So, my friend, if you want to rekindle the flames of passion so your team will remain engaged, begin at the beginning. Build intimacy."
Julie Christiansen

"I invite and encourage leaders to open your mind to the notion that strategic business decisions must intentionally include the people factors at all stages. When we do this, the result is increased productivity and profits and an improved image of the employer brand."

Michelle Bush

"Look after the pennies and the dollars will take care of themselves."
Unknown

"Be sure to center your decisions around humanity. Be a leader that is a strategic thinker and an intuitive listener, strong yet nurturing, brave yet tolerant, empathetic yet authentic."
Aline Ayoub

"The definition of insanity is doing the same thing over and over and expecting different results."
Albert Einstein

"People listen with their emotions. Emotion colours how they interpret facts and generates the energy to drive their actions. Understanding emotions, is listening without judgement, and making room for harnessing new ideas."
Aline Ayoub

"If you want to break the cycle, you need to carve out time to sharpen your saw."
Steven Covey

"To attune yourself to your team's feelings, you must get in touch with your own emotions and understand how to express them."
Aline Ayoub

"The dictionary definition of a "corporate shark in a suit" used as a noun is – a greedy, crafty person who takes advantage of others often through dishonesty, extortion and/or deceitful means."
Alexander Lutchin

"Ultimately all roads lead to the final of the seven fundamentals of leadership, achieving results. Leaders who inspire their team, provide purpose and show that it is possible to achieve amazing results and scale to new heights. Being creative, agile, and coming up with great strategies is great but execution surpasses everything."
Sandra Cabral

"Achieving leadership flow is intentional work and takes practice."
Tanya Smith

"*A coaching culture drives engagement, productivity, and accountability. Leaders who are trained as compassionate coaches inspire meaningful conversations to build relationships, create hopefulness, and bridge communication gaps. Winning teams always have a great and trusted coach.*"
Sandra Cabral

"The connection to your purpose and your why is not just a power source to move you towards the future vision of your team or organization, it is the foundation or what one might describe as your North Star or compass to weather any storm i.e., changes and challenges. This North Star supports your character, builds trust, and enables you to build strong relationships."
Crystal-Lee Olson

"It takes years to build a positive culture and very little time to tear it down."
Sandra Cabral

"EQ can be learned and *developed. As a leader it's critical to cultivate." Wendy Woods*

"*Leaders who communicate well, build on trust and respect. Two-way communication is vital to ensure others feel listened to and valued.*

This is a core value that drives innovation and team development for retention and performance. It builds on trust and respect."
    Sandra Cabral

"Being more emotionally aware will help you see what emotions are arising, what produced them, and how they are affecting you and others at work."
    Wendy Woods

"Leadership is not found in a title. It is found in a person's abilities and actions; a person's ability to align, inspire and measure by consistently demonstrating the seven fundamentals of leadership and team engagement..."
    Sandra Cabral

Thank you for reading this Creative Non-Fiction book; all of the contributing thought leaders trust that you have taken away solid actions, tools, and wisdom that will support your success as a leader as well as in all aspects of your life.
    Be Safe and Keep Well,
    Nance MacLeod, Chief Coaching Officer
    Executive Coach Global

REFERENCES

Bauer, C. et al,. (2019). Mindfulness training reduces stress and amygdala reactivity to fearful faces in middle-school children. *Behavioral Neuroscience, 133*(6), 569–585.

Brown, B. (2020, October 26). Brene with Abby Wambach on the New Rules of Leadership. *Dare to Lead Podcast.* Retrieved from https://open.spotify.com/episode/0eRgnFdCcK93WNhzd6e9EL?si=-AiJLs66S6S9cbF9cjjFpg

Career Compass Canada. (2015). *The Seven Fundamentals of Team Engagement and Leadership: Team Building & Leadership Workbook.* Toronto, Career Compass Canada.

Covey, S. (1989). *The Seven Habits of Highly Effective People.* Free Press.

Frei, F.X., Morriss, A. (2020). Begin with Trust: The first step to becoming a genuinely empowering leader. Harvard Business Review, May-June 2020. Retrieved from https://hbr.org/2020/05/begin-with-trust.

Graziosi, D. (2019). *Millionaire Success Habits: the gateway to wealth & prosperity.* Carlsbad, CA: Hay House.

Goleman, D. (1998). Working with emotional intelligence. New York: Bantam Books.

Goleman, D. (n.d.). *What is Emotional Self Awareness?* Kornferry.com. Retrieved from https://www.kornferry.com/insights/articles/what-is-emotional-self-awareness

Goleman, D. (2018). *How Self-Awareness Pays Off.* LinkedIN. https://www.linkedin.com/pulse/how-self-awareness-pays-off-daniel-goleman/

Herwig, U., Kaffenberger, T., Bruhl, A.B. (2010). Self-related awareness and emotion regulation. *NeuroImage*, 50(2):734-41.

Hill, N. (2016). "The Definition of Purpose" quoted from *Think and Grow Rich*. Retrieved from http://simplyknown.com/self-improvement/the-definiteness-of-purpose-napoleon-hill-quote-think-and-grow-rich

Holzel, B., Carmody, J., Vangel, M., Congleton, C., Yerramsetti, S.M., Gard, T., and Lazar, S.W. (2011). Mindfulness Practice Leads to Increases in Regional Brain Gray Matter Density. *Psychiatry Research, 191(1): 36–43.*

Kabat-Zinn, J. (2016). "20-minute Breath Meditation." *Soundcloud.* Retrieved from https://soundcloud.com/user-801302473/week-2-breath-meditation-jon-kabat-zinn-20-minuten-eng

Killingsworth, M. A., & Gilbert, D. T. (2010). A wandering mind is an unhappy mind. *Science*, *330*(6006), 932–932. https://doi.org/10.1126/science.1192439.

Martinengo, G. (2019, October 24). *Top 25 Best Quotes from Why Leaders Eat Last by Simon Sinek*. Retrieved from https://giuseppemartinengo.org/top-25-quotes-from-leaders-eat-last-by-simon-sinek/

Sinek, S. (2019). *Start with why: How great leaders inspire everyone to take action*. London: Portfolio Penguin.

Sinek, S. (2009, September). TEDxPugent Sound: *How great leaders inspire action*. Retrieved from https://www.ted.

com/talks/simon_sinek_how_great_leaders_inspire_action?language=en

Sternberg, R. J. (1986). A triangular theory of love. Psychological Review, 93, 119–135. Referenced from http://www.robertjsternberg.com/love

Sy, T., Cote, S., Saavedra, R. (2005). "The Contagious Leader: Impact of the Leader's Mood on the Mood of Group Members, Group Affective Tone, and Group Processes". *Journal of Applied Psychology, 90(2):295-305.* DOI: 10.1037/0021-9010.90.2.295

NOTES

1. ROAD TRIP TO LEADERSHIP

1. https://hbr.org/2020/05/begin-with-trust
2. Career Compass Canada. (2015). *The Seven Fundamentals of Team Engagement and Leadership: Team Building & Leadership Workbook.* Toronto, Career Compass Canada.
3. https://www.jackierobinson.com/quotes/
4. Career Compass Canada. (2015). *The Seven Fundamentals of Team Engagement and Leadership: Team Building & Leadership Workbook.* Toronto, Career Compass Canada.
5. Career Compass Canada (2015).

3. LEADING WITH EMPATHY:

1. Covey, S. (1989).
2. www.brainyquote.com/quotes/theodore_roosevelt_140484

5. THE EMOTIONALLY AWARE LEADER

1. Goleman, D. (1998).
2. Goleman. (n.d.).
3. Journal of Applied Psychology 90(2)
4. Goleman, D. (2018, January 31).
5. Britta K. Holzel, et al., (2011).
6. Bauer, C. et al,. (2019).
7. Killingsworth, M. A., & Gilbert, D. T. (2010).
8. Kabat-Zin, J. (2016).
9. https://www.brainyquote.com/quotes/viktor_e_frankl_160380
10. Kabat-Zinn, Jon. (2016).
11. Herwig, Uwe et al., (2010).

6. LOVING LEADERSHIP

1. http://www.robertjsternberg.com/love

7. CONNECTION TO YOUR PURPOSE AND YOUR WHY

1. Sinek, S. in Martinengo (2019).
2. Graziosi, D. (2019).
3. Hill, N. (2016).
4. Brown, B. (2020).
5. Sinek, S. (2009).

ABOUT THE CONTRIBUTORS
IN ORDER OF APPEARANCE

Richard Koroscil, C. Dir.
President and CEO, **KORLON** Strategic Services Inc. A graduate of Durham University, Richard is a senior Aviation executive, and a Chartered Director with 39 years in both the public and private sectors in Canada and Internationally. In 2012 he retired as President/CEO for the Hamilton International Airport.

His career portfolio also includes President and CEO Ontario Chamber of Commerce, Vice President for

Vancouver Airport Services (YVRAS) and the Vancouver International Airport Authority. In these executive roles he was responsible for the privatization, transfer and operating performance of 15 airports in 6 countries including the integration of the YVRAS global family of airports and the branding of the YVRAS product and services. As part of these privatizations he has provided operational direction and coordination for more than a dozen new air terminal building projects and associated airport infrastructure valued at more than $1 Billion USD. Richard was also the President and Director of a number of YVRAS subsidiary companies and former Vice-Chair of the ACI (Airports Council International), Pacific Region and member of the ACI World Facilitation Committee.

Richard sits on the boards of Hamilton Health Sciences and the McMaster Institute of Transportation and Logistics. He is past Chair of the Hamilton United Way 2012 campaign, the Hamilton Chamber of Commerce and the Southern Ontario Gateway Council and Telling Tales. He has served on the Boards of Metrolinx, the Ontario Chamber of Commerce, the Hamilton Immigration Partnership Council, St. Joseph's Hospital Foundation, and Theatre Aquarius. He also serves on Mohawk Colleges Aviation Advisory Council and Chairs the Bay Area Climate Change Council and MIP Connects.

He has also served as a strategic advisor to Hamilton Mayors and Provincial Ministers of Transport.

Sandra Cabral, CHRL
Forward-thinking Positivity Champion with Executive Coach Global

Chapter 1, *The Seven Fundamentals of Leadership*, takes the reader on a retrospective road trip with a few unexpected but ultimately rewarding twists and turns. From early role models through to challenging role reversals, lessons emerge that underscore the key values of trust and respect. In introducing the proprietary leadership development model of Executive Coach Global/Career Compass Canada, the author uses relatable examples to demonstrate how the application of a simple methodology can help every leader maximize their capabilities and achieve results. Along the way, it encourages open-mindedness and promotes the value of leadership rather than management.

On the foundation of over twenty years of progressive Human Resources experience, Sandra is a passionate developer and advocate of people and culture solutions that redefine the relationships between organizational stakeholders. In environments of labour unrest and competitive markets, she has successfully introduced respect-based solutions that build strong leadership and resilient partnerships.

LinkedIn - https://www.linkedin.com/in/sandracabral/

Certified Human Resources Leader | Member, Alternative Dispute Resolution Institute

Alexander Lutchin, BA, APR
CEO with Executive Coach Global

Surviving the Sharks in Suits gives credence to the truism that people don't leave jobs – they leave bosses. It presents a powerful lesson in building well-rounded leadership presence that Robert K. Smith wished he had learned earlier in his career.

To make the leap from being walked out the door on a sunny June morning to transforming his life through learning took courage, conviction and an open mind. A technically sound performer, Robert did not understand the importance of vertical relationships. He needed to be coached along a path to self-awareness, identifying blind spots, refining communication, and creating a culture of inspiration. He needed to grow and develop as an effective, agile and intentional leader.

In relaying this all-too-common scenario, Alexander Lutchin shares concrete advice to shore up the soft skill gap and pre-empt executive pitfalls. With his history of high-profile corporate transformations and years of expertise developing high-performance teams, he has supported countless individuals and organizations to achieve their full potential through alignment, accountability and shared vision.

LinkedIn: https://www.linkedin.com/in/alexanderlutchin/

Accredited in Public Relations | Coaching Certificate, Case Western Reserve University, Weatherhead School of Management | CEO of Career Compass Canada and Executive Coach Global

Aline Ayoub, BA
High-energy Engagement Champion with Executive Coach Global

Chapter 3, *Leading with Empathy*, chronicles the juxtaposition of time-honoured values within the most current of contexts: the unexpected global pandemic of 2020. A senior executive faced with adapting to a dramatically changing business climate confronts the urgent need to rewire his leadership style.

If ever there was a critical moment in history for business leaders to learn to act with empathy while remaining authentic, that time is now. The insights shared in this chapter will help you to overcome your fears of proximity to your team and provide you with powerful tools, advice and models to champion engagement.

A seasoned career mentor, Aline brings sensitivity and strength to this story while driving home her belief that caring for people is central to leadership success. Her extensive work with senior executives generates sharp focus to the importance of finely tuned Emotional Intelligence as a cornerstone of powerful, effective stewardship.

LinkedIn: https://www.linkedin.com/in/alineayoub/

Award-winning Leadership Coach | Certified Myers-Briggs Practitioner | Avid Blogger and Author | French-English Bilingual

Michele Bush, BA, CHRP, CCP
Mother of Re-invention with Executive Coach Global

In Chapter 4, *Unlearning Learned Behaviour*, we meet a

Finance Executive who discovers the value in re-thinking how she once made business decisions. This story shows us how different the outcomes can be when we consciously consider the employee impacts.

It is a journey of self-analysis and exploration that ultimately demonstrates how strategic, thoughtful leadership behaviour can enrich team morale, productivity and employer reputation – factors that drive benefits directly to the bottom line.

Michele is an avid promoter of deliberate transformation. On the power of a 30-year career in HR, Michele re-invented herself becoming a Career Coach and Business Advisor, inspiring her clients to acknowledge their abilities and potential. As an independent consultant, she trains aspiring HR professionals, increasing their influence and confidence. As part of her own evolution, she stepped out of her comfort zone and began acting, at the age of 52!!

LinkedIn: https://www.linkedin.com/in/michbush/

Certified Coach Practitioner | Adult Educator and Certified Facilitator | CHRP

Wendy Woods, MBA, CPCC, PCC
Mindfulness Pioneer with Executive Coach Global
Emotionally Intelligent Leader, Chapter 5, deconstructs the concept of Emotional Intelligence for a Sales Director who,

despite her in-depth technical expertise, falls short on inspiring her team to deliver top performance. After an inventory, EQ-i 2.0, reveals that her Emotional Self-Awareness is her lowest competency, she embarks on a quest to identify and manage her emotions, improve her presence and deal with the challenges of leadership.

The reader learns how self-awareness is the cornerstone of EI and to what extent it affects those around us. As the Sales Director commits to a plan of daily mindfulness activities, she brings about a shift in thinking, planning and ultimately control of the impact of her actions.

Wendy Woods has been working for decades with business leaders to step beyond technical excellence and explore the emotional aspect of guiding others to engage and excel. A seasoned advocate of mindfulness – a technique that has been scientifically proven to boost self-awareness even after a limited number of sessions – she is passionate about injecting greater resilience, mindfulness and EI into the workplace.

LinkedIn - https://www.linkedin.com/in/wendyjwoods/

Certified Professional Co-Active Coach | Certificate in Transformative Mindfulness Methods | Professional Certified Coach

Julie A. Christiansen, MA, RP
Communication and Change Agent with Executive Coach Global

The analogy of a white-water rafting adventure comes alive in Chapter 6, *Loving Leadership*. The story presents the value of applying a well-honed leadership model as a tool to build trust, passion and commitment in any kind of team.

Have you ever wondered how an activity that is dangerous and potentially deadly became something many would put on their bucket list? The secret lies in the skill and the proficiency of the guides and their ability to put people at ease, quickly teach them how to work together not just to survive the journey, but to enjoy it.

Julie Christiansen positions you at the helm of your own vessel, challenging you to embrace the principles of Loving Leadership as you guide your own team. She shares her passion to leverage people and organizations into radical, positive, lasting change, following her mission to propel others towards greatness through individual executive coaching, group workshops, seminars, therapy, or keynote speeches.

LinkedIn: https://www.linkedin.com/in/juliechristiansen

MA in Counselling Psychology | Registered Psychotherapist | Conflict Resolution in the Workplace | Anger Resolution Coach | Creator of Anger Solutions™ Program

Crystal-Lee Olson, MA
Inspirational Dream Builder with Executive Coach Global

Chapter Seven, *Connection to Your Purpose & Why*, traces the revitalization of a business professional struggling with disengagement and self-doubt. In order to emerge from the abyss and unlock her true potential as a leader, she explores and embraces a structured system of Mindset > Strategy > Action.

The underpinning premise of this story is that truly understanding one's purpose and clearly articulating the *Why* of one's vocation are key factors in any success formula. Follow our heroine as she discovers the connection to her purpose using insights, tools and actions that will become her – and your – guideposts to building outstanding teams and organizations.

Crystal-Lee offers these insights on the foundation of 15 years of experience as an entrepreneur backed by 20 years' experience in sales, business development, training, and teaching. Her passion is developing and delivering training and coaching programs to teams and leaders to positively impact performance, career transition and employee engagement.

LinkedIn: https://www.linkedin.com/in/crystalyolson/

MA, Leadership Development | Certified DreamBuilder Accelerator and Transformational Coach | Award-winning Business Development Professional | Fanshawe College Faculty Member

Nance MacLeod, PCC, CEC
Chief Coaching Officer with Executive Coach Global

In Chapter Eight, *Courageous Leadership*, we follow the career trajectory of a financial services professional from her non-auspicious foray into a male-dominated business arena through to glass-ceiling-shattering executive presence.

In relating the story, Nance MacLeod focuses on two key traits – Courage and Tenacity – that underpin this executive's success. She summarizes and imparts six important lessons that you can apply in your own day-to-day to help you face decision making, problem solving and conflict resolution with confidence and purpose.

The wisdom shared in this chapter comes from Nance's more than thirty years of real-life experience as a professionally trained executive and leadership coach. On the foundation of her some 10,000 hours of corporate, group and one-on-one coaching with more than 1,500 executives, she reveals a deep understanding of patterns and tendencies, obstacles and pitfalls, strengths and finesse. Nance will have you sharing her belief that acting with courage gives hope even when hope may not seem obvious.

LinkedIn: https://www.linkedin.com/in/nancemacleod/

Certified Executive Coach | PROSCI Change Practitioner Specialist |
Enterprise Change Management Practitioner |
Corporate Culture Strategist | Master Career Coach

Tanya Smith, CIDC
Idea Igniter with Executive Coach Global

Chapter Nine, *Leadership Flow*, takes us on a quest to become a conscious leader. Using a three-step process, Jackson – our protagonist – advances through a phase of self awareness in order to understand the impact of his behaviour on others and ultimately begin acting from a place of intention.

Jackson's progress underscores the relevance of this style of leadership to building effective, efficient, and enjoyable workplaces and teams.

In describing the journey, Tanya Smith draws on her experience from the past ten years spent working with leaders in various industries, helping them become more present and adaptable leaders. She includes a collection of coaching exercises at the end of the story to support the reader in integrating Reflection, Intention and Action into their own leadership development.

LinkedIn: https://www.linkedin.com/in/tanya-smith-integraldevelopmentcoach/

Certified Integral Development Coach | Certified DiSC and EI Assessment Practitioner | Certified Action Learning Coach

ABOUT EXECUTIVE COACH GLOBAL

Executive Coach Global (ECG) is a premier leadership development, executive coaching, and search firm. ECG also offers a wide range of specialized strategic support including managing change and diversity, equity, and inclusion for a range of organizations across all sectors. Our professional coaches have deep experience working with leaders at all levels of management and C-suite to achieve their highest potential. In particular, we provide solutions for the development of leaders either in an existing role or leaders preparing to take on more responsibility.

We work with teams to help them engage with each other, breaking down silos to increase collaboration and performance to achieve goals and growth. All of our international coaches are members of ICF and have various levels of accreditation. Our Chief Coaching Officer ensures the highest quality of delivery and professionalism. Executive Coach Global offers a vast range of assessments including psychometrics, trust analysis, leadership development, culture development, 360's and more, to help quantify and guide the learning process. We have the right assessment

ABOUT EXECUTIVE COACH GLOBAL

tools to support the development process and help us understand client gaps, strengths, and opportunities. Coaching is available in multiple languages.

Executive Coach Global | Cornerstone Toronto is a partner firm of the Cornerstone International Group, bringing together a talented team of executive search consultants and executive coaches serving clients at home and around the world with a vast network of resources. ECG's sister company, Career Compass Canada, provides comprehensive strategic people and culture solutions and career transition support.

Please visit our website:
www.executivecoachglobal.com

Find us on social media:

LinkedIn: **https://www.linkedin.com/company/executive-coach-global**

Facebook: **https://www.facebook.com/executivecoachglobal**

Instagram: @Executivecoachglobal

Twitter: @executivecoac13